Where Spirits Roam but God Reigns

By Annette McManigle

Where Spirits Roam But God Reigns

By Annette McManigle

Unless otherwise noted, Scripture quotations are from the Holy Bible, New International Version. Copyright © 1973, 1978, 1984, International Bible Society.

Scripture quotations marked NKJV are from the Holy Bible, New King James Version. Copyright © 1982 Thomas Nelson, Inc.

Scripture quotations marked KJV are from the King James Version of the Bible.

Scripture quotations marked NLT are from the Holy Bible, New Living Translation. Copyright © 1996 by Tyndale House Publishers, Inc., Wheaton, IL 60189.

ISBN: 978-1-61565-109-2

Third printing 2011

Dedication

I would like to dedicate this book to my wonderful gifted husband, Scott. You inspire me, love me and faithfully go where God calls you, and are our family's spiritual leader. It is a privilege to be your co-worker and wife for all these years. God blesses me through you daily!

I am also dedicating this book to our four children Daniel, Joel, Seth and Bethany who have joyfully worked alongside us in the ministry. These stories were originally written as a testimony to each of you of God's grace, love and amazing work of which you were a part of even though you were often too small to understand the full picture of God's mighty work. I hope you will see God's amazing faithfulness and grace through these stories, and continue to glorify God with your lives.

Acknowledgements

First and foremost, all praise, honor and glory goes to God. For without Him, there would be no gospel, evangelism, or mission's work of any kind and we'd all still be dead in our trespasses and sins. The things that have been written in this book are meant to be a testimony to the greatness and faithfulness of God and not man.

Secondly, we praise God for New Tribes Mission and the work that He has done and is doing through them around the world. We know of no other organization that seeks to prepare its people to the extent that New Tribes does or one that has defined the end goal so clearly. We shudder to think what kind of missionaries we would have become, or the job we would have done teaching God's word to the Pwo Karen, had we not received NTM's training and the ongoing direction and input from its leaders.

We praise God for the great co-workers that He blessed us with through the years; Harry & Audrey Beard, Barry & Cathy Richards, Mike & Leann Moody and several others who were involved in support rolls for our team. Like all teams that are made up of fallen human beings, we had our share of ups and downs together, but God also blessed us with many great memories. Thank you for your love, patience, understanding and forgiveness through the years. What a blessing it was to join our hearts together to be used by God in doing an "eternal work" in the hearts and lives of the Karen people.

We also praise God for the faithful prayer and financial supporters that co-labored together with us all those years to see the Northern Pwo Karen reached with the gospel and a church established among them; Reston Bible Church, Forreston Grove Church, Fellowship Bible Church, Rich and Evelyn DeVries, Bob & Sandy Varney, Jeff & Nancy Mahmot, Ray & Ruth Ann Keating, Sonny & Dorene Branning, Donald & Beth Browning, Bob & Leisa Shull, Pat & Lyle Moore, and our parents, siblings and other relatives. You have heard these stories through the years, and as you read them again, we pray that your hearts will be gripped afresh with the realization of how blessed and privileged we've been to have been "co-workers together with God." May God bless all of you 100-fold!

We also want to thank the editor, Tom Gill, and the New Tribes Mission team of editors and writers as well as Macon Hare who saw potential in the story and worked to refine it and publish it for others to be blessed by the faithfulness of God through these stories. The network of friends and family who helped in both inspiring me to continue writing as well as reading and editing the stories is long, but are instrumental in the completion of the book. A big thank you to my aunt Doris for giving me the idea in the first place, my mom for saving all our letters, Deb, Christiane and Cheryl for getting me started with their expertise in story flow and ideas. Thank you to Elaine, Sandy, Janice & Sara for reading and editing my very rough drafts, I'm sure it was a struggle at times. Thank you.

Table of Contents

Chapter 1

Too Late

Quickly I drove into the small mountain village in Northern Thailand and parked our four-wheel drive truck in the midst of the scattered little huts. Audrey and I hurriedly got out, as did the tribal man who had come with us riding in the back of the truck. Wasting no time, he led us to one of the huts where a small crowd was gathered on the rickety wooden porch.

Following our guide, we climbed up the two-rung ladder onto the porch. Both Audrey and I abandoned our flip-flops among the sea of shoes and ducked under the thatched overhang of the roof as we entered the bamboo house. Our eyes needed a moment to adjust as the only light that entered the hut came between the cracks in the walls, casting beams of sunlight through the swirling smoke and onto the floor. The smell of wood smoke from the cooking fire was thick in the house, yet my nose was still able to pick up the distinct odor that marked a new delivery.

A woman, exhausted from giving birth, was sitting on the floor next to her husband. Her shoulders were slouched and her legs were stretched out in front of her. Her hand-woven skirt and the flooring where she sat were soiled from the delivery. As she took note of our presence, her eyes brightened and she smiled weakly, relieved that we had come.

"Come and help her!"

We were missionaries living in the village of Maepae (May Pay) in northern Thailand. Our team included Audrey and her husband, Harry, Cathy and her husband, Barry, my husband, Scott, and me. Earlier that day while Audrey and I were home-schooling our children together, a man had come to us with an urgent plea: "My sister had a baby last night, and she still has not delivered the placenta. Come and help her!" The man spoke in his native tongue, which we had learned and could understand fairly well by this time.

"Which village?" I asked.

"Xwee Muu (Pig Creek)," he replied.

We knew this village was at least a thirty-minute drive from Maepae. Both our husbands had gone to town earlier that morning and had not yet returned. Neither Audrey nor I had done much driving on these rough mountain roads, as we had been happy to leave that up to our husbands. Now, however, this man needed our help

Audrey and I discussed our options and made a plan. Audrey took the children down the hill to Barry and Cathy's house to see if Cathy would be willing to take care of the six of them until our return. She willingly agreed. Meanwhile, I gathered some medical supplies and tried to think of everything we could possibly need. Both Audrey and I wondered that morning what we would encounter.

Scott had taught me how to drive the truck, but I could feel my back and neck tensing up as I carefully drove along the narrow, winding dirt road. Remembering his instructions, I had locked the hubs before we left Maepae and shifted into four-wheel-drive as we approached the steep hills so that we could ascend slowly and carefully. Needless to say I was very thankful that it was the dry season and that the roads were not slippery.

Evidence of the hard rains several months before still remained. Deep gullies and ruts squiggled down the trail, eventually finding their way to the side and running over the edge. The road twisted and turned around the sides of the mountains with steep drop-offs on one side or the other. A quick glance at the adjacent hillsides revealed steep rice fields being cleared in preparation for the coming year's crop. People working on the steep inclines with machetes and small hand tools looked like specks in the vast spaces yet to be cleared. Small clusters of full grown trees stood between fields or in areas of unfarmed land. Every now and then, a small cluster of huts marked another village.

Forty minutes later we arrived at Xwee Muu. It was a typical tribal village like those found all over these mountains; small, with one-room huts built on stilts and topped with thatched roofs.

Would she make it?

After settling on the floor near the young mother, Audrey and I began asking her questions in order to assess the situation:

"When was the baby born," I asked?

"When the roosters started crowing this morning."

"Have you had contractions since then?"

"No."

Having encountered this situation several times in the years we lived there, I massaged her abdomen to help her deliver the placenta naturally, but nothing happened.

"Have you lost a lot of blood?" Audrey asked.

"Yes, a lot," she replied.

Since we were unsure how much "a lot" meant, we examined her skirt and then went down under the house to check the ground beneath her. The cracks in the floor had provided a way for the blood to escape, but even though the dirt was stained, it was apparent that the dogs had been there, and any evidence we hoped to find had been lost.

Audrey and I knew the mother could have been bleeding internally, and she definitely appeared to be getting weak, so after going back inside the house we discussed how to proceed. To reach the hospital would take almost three hours and we wondered if we could do it. Furthermore, would she make it?

We decided the only alternative was to try getting her to the hospital; nothing could be done for her in the village. Thankfully, the woman's husband agreed. I hurried up the hill to get the truck and backed it up to the porch. Audrey and the woman's husband each took an arm to help her stand and then made their way slowly to the truck. The couple's teenage daughter met them with a straw mat and blankets draped over her arm so that her mother could have a more comfortable place on the hard metal surface. The husband sat with his back against the truck cab holding his wife's head and shoulders in his lap.

The family's newborn baby boy was wrapped in a dirty cloth and cradled in his older sister's arms. Though no more than fifteen years old, she was accustomed to caring for her siblings while her parents worked in the rice fields all day. With her mother now settled in the back of the truck, she climbed in the cab with the baby sleeping contentedly in her arms.

Audrey rode in back with the woman and her husband in case they needed her assistance. I settled in behind the wheel and whispered a prayer: "Lord, please, help us now. Give us safety and strength. Please, save this woman's life, and give us wisdom."

As we pulled away from the house, I tried to drive carefully and keep the truck from bumping and rocking, but it was no use.

The ground was rough and the incline steep. Friends and family watched helplessly from the couple's porch as we carried her away toward modern medical care.

The trip took longer on our return to Maepae because I was driving slow, trying to miss all the holes and ruts in the road to keep from jarring our precious cargo. By the time we reached our house, Audrey was concerned because the woman's breathing seemed labored. With just a glance, I understood Audrey's worry. The woman was becoming increasingly pale and was drifting in and out of consciousness. Her eyes were closed and she was not responding to our questions.

I stopped for a brief moment to get a small plastic pipe to help keep her mouth open and airway free. Then I jumped back into the truck and tried to drive a bit faster. The road improved slightly but it would still be nearly an hour before we reached the main highway, from there the hospital was still another hour away.

Too Far — Too Slow — Too Late

Audrey was trained as a nurse so she knew how to handle this situation much better than I did. That we could work as a team in this emergency was a great blessing. I tried to drive faster, but there were times the road was just too rough to keep up the pace and I had to slow down again.

About two miles outside our village, I heard Audrey call me from the back.

"Annette, stop!" she said.

With tears in her eyes, she tried to resuscitate the woman again and again but to no avail. Feeling for a pulse, she found none. Finally, Audrey looked up at me and said, "We've lost her, Annette. She's gone."

I couldn't believe it. *"This can't be,"* I thought.

The girl, still holding her brother, had climbed out of the cab and was standing beside the truck bed. Realizing that her mother was gone, her eyes welled up and tears began running down her cheeks. As Audrey climbed out of the back of the truck to get into the cab, the girl pushed the baby into her arms and turned her face away to hide her tears. Audrey, now holding the baby got into the truck while the girl climbed into the back to be with her dad.

The woman's husband had tears in his eyes as he sat holding his wife's body. Death had won, and there was nothing we could do but return to their village.

Since turning back was our only option, I had to drive farther down the trail to find a place wide enough to turn around. We rode along in silence, Audrey studying the sweet face of the tiny baby in her arms, both of us fighting to hold back tears. I couldn't help but think about this woman's soul, separated from God forever. She never had the opportunity to hear God's Word and know the truth of salvation through Jesus Christ.

Deep Sadness

The trail we were on passed the outer edge of Maepae. As I was about to move on, the husband slapped the side of the truck and signaled for me to stop. As I slowed he jumped out and came up to the window.

"I need to ask permission from the spirit-headman to return to my village. I will need to pay a fine for taking a dead body through their village," he explained and then he hurried off.

We had heard that it was taboo to carry a corpse through another village. The people believed the spirits would become angry and that sickness or trouble would befall many families. Therefore, the husband would have to make restitution for breaking taboo or be blamed for the misfortunes of other people.

The mid-day sun beat down on us for what seemed like hours before the man returned. His wife's lifeless body lay in the truck covered with a blanket, his young daughter sat near her sobbing quietly, and his newborn baby was sleeping in Audrey's arms.

Though relieved to be headed back to Xwee Muu, I was deeply saddened to be driving a hearse instead of an ambulance. My heart ached for the whole family but especially for the young girl. I had no words with which to comfort her. I was unable to tell her that she would see her mother again in heaven or that her mother was in a much better place, or that her pain was gone. I felt the hopelessness, the emptiness and the grief of the situation.

The only sounds in the cab were the baby's occasional cries for nourishment, which none of us could give him. The adrenalin rush had subsided and now I was drained, my body aching for food. I felt light headed, my hands shook, and nausea began to sweep over me from missing lunch. By the time we reached the village my head was pounding. I told Audrey I would have to sit in the truck while the family unloaded the body because I was too drained to help. I couldn't do any more.

As soon as the first house came into sight the husband began wailing loudly as if to announce our arrival. The sound of his cries echoed through the village and made the lump in my throat swell as I suppressed my emotions. The villager's cries began loud and then bounced up and down in pitch as their breath ran out and they paused to fill their lungs. Then the wailing would begin again. The familiar cry aroused everyone's attention as the entire village came out of their houses and off their porches to join in the death chorus. There was nothing more to say; the sound said it all.

Surrounded by such profound grief, I felt like I had let them all down. Instead of returning with a new mother and healthy newborn, I drove in with a lifeless body covered with a blanket. Audrey and I fought back the tears as many others joined the widower, erupting in loud wailing.

Teetering on the Edge of Exhaustion

Once more I backed the truck up to the porch. Quivering and sweating I stayed in the truck while Audrey got out. I assumed the family's relatives would help the husband get his wife's body out of the truck, but I was wrong. He knew that if Audrey and I helped him, he would not owe the fees due to anyone who touched his wife's dead body.

Emotionally and physically exhausted, I tried my best to ignore his plea for help. However, after a few moments I left the truck and, with legs trembling, climbed into the back of the truck to help. The three of us lifted the body out of the truck and then up the rickety ladder onto the porch. I could not believe how heavy it was.

As we lifted the woman's body, the blanket she was wrapped in began to slip from our grip. To keep from dropping her, we had to lay her down on the porch to regain our hold. Then, moving in unison we ducked under the low roof and into the house.

Weak and shaking, I was ready to sit down; I had done my part. But the husband needed more.

"Help me wrap her for burial," he said.

He pulled down a woven rattan mat from the low rafters just above our heads and laid it on the floor next to his wife's body. Then we helped him move her onto the mat.

"Take her bracelets off," he told us.

Without a word, Audrey and I began taking them off and laying them in a pile. As I lifted her limp arm and began bending the bracelets to get them off I could hardly believe I was doing this. Her flesh was still slightly warm from all the exposure to the sun since her death, but the weight of it was unlike anything I had ever felt.

Audrey and I each worked on an arm until we had removed at least thirty bracelets each.

While we had been busy with the bracelets, the man had been searching through his wife's things and found a skirt and shirt that she had woven but never worn. She had made them to wear when her old garments were worn out, torn, or perhaps for a special occasion such as a wedding. Young and active, she probably never thought they would be used for her burial.

"Take the clips out of her hair," the husband instructed us. I had a hard time looking at his wife's face while I worked, not because I was afraid, but because of the sadness that filled my heart. That morning I had talked to her, and now her soul was separated from God for all of eternity.

When we removed all of her decorative necklaces we helped the husband change his wife's clothes. Then he took a coin from a bag, placed it on her forehead and chattered a few words. Some sort of blessing, I presumed.

Wailing broke out from time to time as we worked while their fifteen year old daughter watched at the doorway. We helped the man fold the ends of the mat over his wife's head and feet and then we folded the sides of the mat over her body, tucking it under her so it would stay. Then he began to cry loudly again as if to say good bye.

Tears stung my eyes. I had never been faced with death in this way, and I could not shake the sense of loss and despair in death without Christ. It lay heavy on my heart.

What About the Baby?

We walked out onto the porch where an aunt was holding the baby. With all that had been happening, it was the first time that the baby's health had entered our minds. Audrey picked him up again and looked him over. His umbilical cord looked good and his color was good.

Audrey and I began to wonder what the father was thinking about his new son. We knew that it was extremely rare for tribal women to take another woman's baby. And formula was not affordable or accessible to them.

Audrey and I knew of an American missionary family who wanted to adopt, so we talked about what to do in English to ensure that no one could understand. It seemed cold to ask the father about taking his baby just after losing his wife, but we hoped we could. The father would have to initiate this, however, so after making sure the baby was healthy we handed him back and set out to leave.

The father stopped us and asked, "What about the baby? Can't you take him? What will I do with him? I have nothing to give him, no way to care for him."

"We have friends who will take him if you want," Audrey told him.

"If you want them to take him, they will raise him as their own son. They will not return him to you when he is old enough to eat solid food," I added.

"Will one of you take him so that I can see him more often," he inquired?

"No, it will not be us, but friends of ours. They are foreigners like us and they will take good care of him and raise him as their own child," I replied.

"Okay, take him with you and let your friends raise him, I cannot, he will die here."

Audrey took the little one from his aunt who was holding him out for her to take. Then we got in the truck and pulled away from the house. As we drove away we could hear the wails of family and friends as they grieved the loss of their loved one.

What hopelessness dwells here! I thought. The young children had experienced more death than I had in my entire life. However, in the midst of my grief I felt the Holy Spirit speak to my heart, "This is why you are here." He was reminding me once again of the purpose for our living among these precious people:

> *We have come to bring the hope of Christ to these people. We have come to share Christ who is the Way: the only way to God the Father; the Truth: the truth that sets us free from sin and death; and the Life: eternal life for our souls, and spiritual abundance during our time on this earth.*

I looked over to the little newborn baby who had just fallen asleep in Audrey's arms. Thinking of his future filled me with hope. This tiny little boy was being taken out of this dark and hopeless place to be adopted into a family where he would be taught God's Word. I was reminded of my own adoption into God's family and how it had set me free from sin and despair. "Thank you, Lord," I whispered, as I drove the winding road toward home.

The events of the day had taken their emotional toll on both Audrey and me. I was greatly relieved to be able to share the experience with my husband, Scott, when he returned home. However that night when my body was finally able to rest, my mind did not. As I lay under the mosquito net, listening to the crickets chirping and a village dog barking, my mind drifted back to how God had originally given me the desire to spend my life in one of the most remote places of the earth. God has sent me to bring hope to tribal people that might otherwise never know Him and experience forgiveness and hope in their lives.

Chapter 2

Called to Share "God's Talk"

Twelve years earlier when I was seventeen, I volunteered to go with a small international group (New Tribes Mission, Summit) to assist missionary families with some work projects deep in the jungles of Papua, New Guinea. After short stops in Port Moresby and the mission headquarters in Goroka, the group boarded a small single engine airplane three at a time and flew out over the jungle. My father was a pilot so I was comfortable in this type of aircraft and totally enjoyed the sights below.

From Goroka, we flew over lush mountainous areas. Every now and then we would see a small group of brown grass-roofed huts in a clearing with snake-like trails leading out from the village and disappearing under the thick green foliage of the trees. Rivers wound around the hills and through the carpet of green trees.

We traveled by air for about two hours to reach our destination with nothing but forest beneath us the entire time. The steeper mountains had long given way to rolling hills in the lower elevations when our pilot informed us that we were drawing near our destination. Small villages could be seen from time to time, usually situated near the rivers. Often just a thread of white smoke making its way through the tree canopy revealed human presence below.

Like the rest of the group, I wondered what it would be like to meet tribal people and witness first hand how they lived. As our little aircraft began the descent we were able to get a bird's eye view of the layout of the village where we would be staying for the next four weeks. The grass airstrip ran parallel to the river with a cluster of small huts sandwiched between. The native people and the missionaries had heard the plane coming and stood at the edge of the runway to welcome us. Landing on the grass strip proved to be a bumpy ride, but the pilot managed it with great skill.

My Name is Gilimase

One particularly hot afternoon a couple of weeks into our stay, several native visitors appeared in the village. One of the men, who seemed to be the leader, asked the missionary to call all of us together because he had something to say. Girded around his waist was a wide belt made of reeds with dried grass hanging from the front as a covering. His feet were bare, very thick and tough, and covered with dried mud from the long walk through the jungle. The men had journeyed four days over steep mountains and through jungle swamps to contact the missionaries.

We stood in a circle while the heat of the mid-day sun burned down on us, quietly listening to each word our visitor spoke. One of the missionaries translated as the man told his story:

My name is Gilimase. I am a Bisorio from a distant village. The white man that lives here is teaching God's talk to the Bisorio in this village, but we live too far away and we cannot come here to listen to all of God's talk. We have been told by our Bisorio friends in this village that when we die we will go to hell if we do not hear God's talk. We need someone to come to our village and tell us these things.

Gilimase's skin was very dark and shiny from the sweat of walking through the jungle. He had beads made of white shells around his neck and his hair stood straight up on the top of his head with a few feathers sticking out. Several white strands of beads formed a band around the base of his hair which covered only the crown of his head. His wide nose was pierced and from each hole extended a long, skinny stick that reminded me of upside down antennas.

Gilimase held a bundle of sticks in his hand, each about six inches long. Though I had seen them right away, it was only when he raised them in front of him that I realized they held some kind of meaning. Slowly, he drew one stick out of the bunch and held it up for all of us to see. Then he said: *"My brother, Wadu, will die and go to hell..."* he paused and then tossed the stick to the ground at our feet, *"...if no one comes to tell us God's talk."*

He pulled out another stick and held it up. *"My wife Bilamay will die and go to hell, if no one comes."* Then he tossed the stick to the ground.

"Malodo, my son, will die and go to hell." Another stick hit the ground at our feet.

One after another, Gilimase held up sticks calling out the names of people he knew and loved. Then he would toss them to the ground representing another person who would go to hell. When he was finished, the ground was littered with sticks, each one representing someone who had no hope of eternal life unless they were told the truth of the gospel. After Gilimase and the other visitors left we silently gathered up the sticks, his words playing over and over in our minds.

From Adventure to Calling

Weeks earlier when flying in over the jungle, I remembered seeing the little villages that dotted the mountains. "People who live in those villages will pass away without even a chance to hear the truth of God's Word," I thought. "They will spend eternity without God and will be punished for their sins because they did not know that Jesus offered His life to acquit them from judgment." I shivered at the thought. I had traveled here to have an adventure and it had met all my expectations, but there was no denying that the events of that day impressed a permanent mark on my heart and life.

When darkness fell that evening, I quickly said good night to my friends in order to have some time on my own with God. As I lay on my hard mattress under the mosquito net, I prayed...

> *"Lord, thank You for opening my eyes today. I see there is a need for more Christians to go and tell others about You. I pray for Gilimase and his village that someone will go and tell them soon. How heart-wrenching to see his desire yet watch him walk away empty."*

Captivated by the thoughts racing through my head, I lay staring into the dark. Then I felt God's unmistakable presence and heard His voice speak silently to my heart:

> *"Annette, I want you to be a missionary. I want you to take this message of hope and life to people like Gilimase."*

A lump formed in my throat as I thought about what the Lord said. "This is not what I had planned, God! I have one more year of high school, and I want to get a secretarial job after that. I want to start making money, living comfortably near my home and family in Illinois."

My will was fighting with God. This was a wonderful summer excursion, but to stay in a place like this full time was totally out of the question.

Though I felt overwhelmed I could not ignore that still, small voice in my heart that kept saying, *"I have called you, Annette, to be a missionary."* After replaying the scene of Gilimase throwing the sticks on the ground over and over again in my head I finally dozed off and slept peacefully.

The next morning during our devotional time reading the Bible and praying together, we considered Gilimase and his desperate plea. *"Are you going to give him the Gospel,"* one of the team members asked Bob Kennell, the missionary?

Bob explained to all of us that it would take many weeks of teaching for Gilimase to understand the Creator God—who He is and how He provided for mankind to be saved from eternal punishment. He explained…

> *"We start at the beginning of the Bible and teach chronologically, unfolding God's perfect plan of salvation. If we teach this way, they have a firm understanding of God to build their faith upon. Without knowing what God is like and His character through the Old Testament stories, Gilimase would only be confused. If I were to give him the gospel, he would not understand it. He needs much more than that."*

Many in our group shared how God was working in their hearts after what they had witnessed the day before. When it was my turn, I knew I had to tell them about what had happened the night before.

"I feel like God wants me to be a missionary, but I really don't want to. So I'd like to ask you to pray for me. Please pray that if this is what God wants He will give me the desire to do it. Pray that God will change my heart," I pleaded.

Here am I, Lord…Send Me

Over the next several days while working at various jobs, I often prayed that God would alter my thoughts and emotions and that His will would be done. I do not remember a certain time or day that God answered my prayer that my desires would be His desires; it just happened gradually as I kept talking to Him about it. Nevertheless, when I realized what happened I became very excited. The very thing that just days earlier seemed like a burden suddenly thrilled me. I kept thinking, "God wants me to be a missionary. I am ready to go NOW!" In fact, God had changed my feelings about His call for my life so radically that the thought of having to go home, finish school and enroll in mission training almost frustrated me.

A few weeks later when my time in the Bisorio village had come to an end, a very different girl landed at Chicago O'Hare airport. Growing up in a loving Christian home, I had the privilege of knowing God from a very young age. But it was not until I heard Gilimase's plea to bring the message of Jesus to his tribal village that I understood in my heart that many people in this world will never have the chance to hear and be saved unless someone goes to them; someone who takes the time to learn their language and teach them about God and His plan to save them from eternal separation from Him.

God used the trip to New Guinea to transform my life, my goals and my desires. He changed my heart so that I now saw beyond myself to a needy and lost world. God used this particular tribal man to open my eyes to the need for missionaries and to forever change the course of my life.

Now, twelve years later, the memories of my New Guinea experience were still very vivid, and I had no doubt that God had been leading me from the start. On my own, I would have never been able to guess where I would end up and what life as a missionary would really be like.

I was still shaken by the death of the young mother we had tried so desperately to save earlier in the day. Scott's arms around me comforted me, assuring me that we were exactly where God wanted us to be. However, the memory of what had happened made it unmistakably clear how far away Maepae was from all that was familiar to us. "Yes, this place is far off geographically and culturally," I thought, "but the real obstacle we are up against is spiritual."

Gilimase had a strong desire to hear God's Word, and God had orchestrated things in his life so that his heart was prepared to hear the message from the Word of God. He was willing to hike four days through the jungle to seek out those who could tell him what he wanted to know. Scott and I hoped that God had done that same work in the hearts of the Pwo Karen in Maepae and that at least some were ready, even hungering for the Truth, just like Gilimase.

Chapter 3

Finding a Village

After the life-changing trip to New Guinea, God led me to New Tribes Bible School where Scott and I met. There we learned deeper truths of God's Word and grew in our relationship with God and each other, sharing the same burden for spreading the good news of Jesus to remote tribes. Through Scott, God provided me with my best friend, co-worker and spiritual leader. We were married in August 1986.

Throughout our mission training, Scott and I prayed that God would prepare the hearts of the tribal people we would one day reach. We prayed that they would be just like Gilimase and would be ready to hear "God's talk." Though we didn't know where God would send us, we wanted Him to lead us. Scott and I were confident in the fact that God knew where He wanted to use us and that He would make it clear to us as well.

A man's heart plans his way, but the Lord directs his steps. (Proverbs 16:9 NKJV)

As we continued through training, God redirected us several times as we stepped out by faith. At one point we decided to go to Colombia, but God guided us to Thailand instead.

Called and Sent to Thailand

By the time we left for the mission field, we had two boys, eighteen month old Daniel, and Joel, who was only three months old. We arrived in Thailand and spent the next fourteen months in Bangkok learning the Thai language. While there, we earnestly prayed that God would show us which tribe we should go to.

Then God intervened again. We had decided to work with one tribal group, but God steered us to another, the Pwo Karen (Poe Kah-wren) tribe. All along the way we knew we could trust God to take us to the people we had prayed for…those He had already prepared to receive His truth.

At the conclusion of our language study, we moved north to a small town called Maesariang (Maa-sa-ree-ung) where we teamed up with Harry and Audrey Beard and their two boys. We also met Bobby and Addie Storey, seasoned missionaries who had lived among the Pwo Karen people for nine years in the village of Klompae. They had faithfully learned the language and had even begun teaching from the Bible in the village, but there had been little interest.

After nine years of hard work the Storey's and their co-workers were forced to leave because the villagers blamed them (the foreigners) for their animals getting sick and dying. Village leaders felt the harmony of the village spirits was disturbed and the solution was to either move the village away from the missionaries, or have the missionaries move out. The Storey's did not want to leave, but felt it was the best solution since it was obvious the villagers were not ready to listen to the Word of God. So with heavy hearts the team moved out.

Six years had passed since Bobby and Addie Storey had left Klompae, but after many trips back into the area, Bobby began to sense a change of heart among some of the Karen people. Since the Storey's were headed back to Canada for good, he requested that a new team be formed to try once again to take the message of salvation to the area. We, along with the Beard's, made up that new team.

While living in the town of Maesariang, Scott, Harry and Bobby made survey trips to Pwo Karen villages in the area. They were looking for a suitable, strategic village to move into, but more importantly the one that God wanted us to live in. Usually just the men went on the surveys, but there was a village with great potential that Bobby wanted us wives to see too, so we planned a trip to go as couples. When we made this first trip to Maepae, I was eight months pregnant with Seth, our third son.

Bobby and his co-worker, Winston, had visited Maepae many times before while living in the mountains. On one of these trips, the villagers were on edge about a murder that had taken place the night before. The body still lay in the woods where he fell because they were afraid to dispose of it. The people believed that evil spirits lingered near a body when violent death occurred.

Unafraid and wanting to help, Bobby and Winston offered to wrap the man's body and bury it. The offer was instantly accepted, so they buried him in a shallow grave according to the Karen custom. These villagers did not know God. They also didn't know why these two strangers would offer to help them. However, Bobby and Winston knew that God would use this situation for His glory and trusted that God would reveal Himself to the Karen people.

Maepae

The day was already warm even though the sun had just risen and clouds loomed in the distance. Before leaving, we gathered near the motorcycles and prayed together:

> *Lord, we pray You will give us safety as we travel today.*
> *Give us wisdom to know what questions to ask, and lead us*

*to the right people to talk to. We pray You will make it clear
to all of us if this is the village You desire for us to move
into. We also pray You will protect our children while we
are gone. Thank you. In Jesus' name, Amen.*

Leaving our children in the care of a trusted Thai friend, we
mounted the motorbikes and rode out of town up through the
mountains.

We left the paved road about forty-five minutes into our trip.
The dirt road started out fairly good, but the farther we went the
more it worsened. In most places the trail was a rusty red color
consisting of mostly clay. Along the sides of the narrow road, small
hand-cultivated fields produced squash and peanuts as cash crops
for the people of the small Thai settlements along the way. We
passed through four such villages before starting the climb up the
mountain toward Maepae.

Before leaving the valley the road took us between bright green
rice paddy fields full of growing rice. They looked so perfect and
velvety. At the end of the paddy fields we drove up to a fairly long
wooden bridge that crossed over a small river. The bridge deck
had narrow boards running crossways and longer, wider boards
like tracks that ran the entire length of the bridge for truck tires to
follow. The boards had come loose in spots and some of them bowed
upwards where the nails had pulled through, banging back down
as we rode across. With all the clapping and clanking, I felt as if the
whole bridge would give way at any second, which made me very
nervous. My pounding heart returned to normal when we reached
solid ground on the other side.

Parting with the last hamlet of civilization, we began the long,
slow ascent into the mountains. The trail grew narrower and the
vegetation along the sides became denser. We crossed through

a shallow winding creek seven or eight times, at one point riding against the current for thirty feet or so before beginning the steep climb up the other side.

Along the way it began to sprinkle and the already difficult trail turned slick. Up and down steep hills we crawled trying to dodge erratic ruts that looked like twisted vines on the road. As we climbed higher and higher, the drop-off on one side of the path got steeper and steeper. Two hours later, with my legs tired from clenching Scott and my big belly sore from the strain and bumping along the trail, we arrived at what seemed the end of the world.

Remote and Primitive

Now this is remote! This is isolated! This is a real tribal village, I thought. I saw the primitive houses, barefoot kids wearing little or nothing, and pigs and chickens foraging around the houses with their young running to keep up.

The villagers must have heard us coming because both sides of the trail were lined with people. Despite our rain gear, we were muddy and wet where the rain coats didn't cover us.

The scene unfolding before our eyes was worth studying. The women and teenage girls adorned their hair with silver clips. Their arms were laden with thick brass bracelets from wrist to bicep with only a space at the elbow that allowed them to bend their arms. Colorfully beaded necklaces by the hundreds hung around their necks, and large holes in their ear lobes were filled with chunky metal studs adorning multicolored yarn earrings. Nearly all the young children were naked. The men wore mostly red, hand woven, shirts, and black or blue cotton trousers.

With the amount of jewelry displayed by the women, it seemed as if they were dressed for a special occasion, but we soon learned that their daily attire included all of these beads and bangles. They work their fields and even sleep wearing them. We were told that the women are so accustomed to their jewelry they are unable to sleep without it.

Through the rain, we could see small bamboo huts with grass roofs. A few scattered houses had tin roofs and hand-sawn lumber on the walls. They were all built up off the ground on stilts with rickety homemade ladders reaching to the mud below. The slope of this mountain village made the houses look somewhat precarious standing on such an uneven landscape. Pot-bellied pigs with their babies and scrawny dogs slept under the houses where it was drier.

Addie had brought some medicine with her which was in great demand. The villagers hovered around as she gave them pills for headaches and other ailments and explained how to take them.

I sure hope that one day we will be able to communicate like her, handing out medicine, getting to know these people, and eventually sharing with them the message of salvation through Jesus, I thought to myself as I watched her at work. Scott and I grinned at each other; we could feel each others' excitement. We wondered if this could be the village that we had been praying about for years.

Our First Meeting

Soon all the medication was gone and we were invited into a nearby house. As we climbed up the ladder into the dark, smoke-filled Karen house, the split bamboo floor flexed and creaked with our weight. The headman of the village and several other Karen men awaited us. Following their lead, we sat down on the floor with everyone else. Bobby had arranged this meeting so he could ask permission for Harry, Audrey, Scott and me to live in this village. He also mentioned that we would bring medicine with us.

To this day, I do not know all the details about what was discussed during this first encounter as only a few words sounded vaguely familiar. It would take months before these foreign sounds would start to make any sense to me.

As the men and Bobby talked back and forth, I surveyed our surroundings. The central item in the house was the firebox around which we sat. The firebox is a square section recessed into the main floor that is packed hard with clay; the fire for cooking is built on top of it. A small fire burning provided just enough light to dimly see once my eyes had adjusted. There were no windows, and the door was only slightly ajar. The smoke had nowhere to go, so it hovered thick above our heads and was more tolerable where we sat on the floor. Three feet above the fire was a platform made of woven bamboo. The legs of the platform were anchored at the four corners of the firebox and made from large stalks of bamboo. Cooking utensils were stored in angular holes made in the side of these legs for easy access. *This must be their drying rack,* I concluded. Blackened corn hung in twos and threes by the dry husk from under the platform, as well as some things I did not recognize. *Maybe some kind of meat cut in strips for drying,* I decided.

As I looked around, I noticed several cooking pots blackened with soot that sat near the wall on a long, narrow bench just a few inches from the floor. There were also dirty, white enamel plates and metal spoons stored there. In one corner of the house, blankets and small pillows lay in a heap. Just above that, clothing was draped over a rope that was strung up across the corner. Near the door a cluster of thick bamboo tubes hung by fibrous strands. Each one was capped with a green leaf fastened with smaller flexible fibers. *Water containers,* I deduced, trying to make sense of our surroundings. One had a small crack part way down and water slowly dripped onto the bamboo floor, quickly disappearing under the house.

From the dripping water, my eye traveled back to the tribal men who continued to talk with Bobby. One of the men had an odd appearance. He had very long black hair arranged all to one side, tied in a ponytail just below and in front of one ear and hanging down over the front of his shoulder. Several silver clips held his hair in place. His lips were painted bright red, and a few red dots were carefully drawn on each cheek. When he smiled, his front top teeth were shiny gold. Addie told us later that eligible teenage boys dressed this way to be attractive. "Beauty is in the eye of the beholder," she said with a grin.

Now We Wait

When the meeting was over, Bobby explained that our request would come before the entire village for discussion at the next village assembly. We would be told of their decision later.

Before leaving, we took some time to walk around the village. The rain still fell and the red clay and sloping terrain made it challenging to keep our feet steady beneath us. Wherever we walked, we saw young girls wearing long, white dresses. Addie and Bobby told us that their dress indicated that they were unmarried. They told us that once these young women become wives, they would wear red shirts and skirts. Sure enough, as we looked around, we saw a lot of women in red. Their hand-woven garments were very colorful and had intricate designs.

Time slipped away so we had to hurry if we wanted to get back to Maesariang before dark. However, our trip down the mountain would be just the first of many adventures on the trail.

We had not ridden very far when Bobby's bike began losing power and leaking gas. With no engine to hold them back, they sped down the hills and then coasted up the next hill as far as they could go. When they slowed to nearly a stop, we would ride up beside them and Scott would put his foot on their foot peg and push as long as we could. I was nervous, but could tell that Scott enjoyed the challenge.

As we neared a small Thai village, Harry and Bobby began to push the broken bike. But the adventure was not yet over. Audrey, who was inexperienced at driving a motorcycle, offered to give Addie a ride the last little way on their bike. They were on a slight incline and Audrey stalled the bike on the first few attempts to start out. To compensate, she gave it too much throttle the next time and let the clutch go too quickly. With a sudden burst of power, the front wheel came up off the ground and Addie landed with a thud on the muddy trail. To our surprise she just lay there laughing hysterically and in no hurry to get up.

Seeing that Addie was obviously unhurt, Audrey, red faced and embarrassed, coaxed her to get up off the ground before more on-lookers gathered. She got up, but decided to walk the rest of the way. We all bunched together under the awning of the tiny make-shift bike shop where Bobby's bike got a temporary fix. Then we finished the ride back home to our kids and much needed showers, arriving just before dark.

Scott and I prayed together that night:

> *God, please help us make the right decision as a team. Lead us and guide us. If this is the village You want us to move into, we pray the village council will decide favorably for us. If these are the people whose hearts You have made ready, then make it clear this is where we should settle. We trust in You to lead us.*

Visions of all we had seen and experienced played through my head as I went to sleep that night.

Chapter 4

Moving

Permission to move into Maepae finally came, though now I don't remember how we heard the news. Nevertheless, when word came Scott and I felt it was the confirmation we had sought from the Lord. After much prayer, our little team agreed this was the place where God was leading us, so we began to make plans for house building and moving.

Seven months after our initial trip to Maepae, Scott began building our house and Harry began working on theirs. My parents came to help for a month, so Scott and Dad rode motorcycles up to the village almost daily and worked. Meanwhile, Mom and I canned food that we would take with us when we moved.

After three months, the day finally came when we could move into the village. We were very excited to finally be moving in to live among the tribe we had prayed God would lead us to.

With our belongings packed in our truck and two other trucks driven by some friends, we started the 2½ hour journey to our new home. Seth, now eight months old, was on my lap while Daniel and Joel, who were two and three, sat in the back seat. The trip started slowly because of the heavy cargo and became even slower when we turned onto the narrow dirt road. We followed the path that wound down into the valley, through several small villages and then back up again on the other side into the mountains.

The road was steep in places, and even though it was now dry and dusty, the evidence of hard rains washing ruts into the surface made for lots of bumps. The trucks rocked back and forth as we crossed over gullies and wash-outs. We traveled along the same trail we had taken before over the rickety wooden bridge and through all the stream crossings, now flowing smaller due to lack of rain.

Maepae

Traveling along, I became lost in thought as we rounded bend after bend going up the mountain. Then, after climbing and winding around for hours on the trail, we arrived at Maepae, about 4,000 feet above sea level.

Wow! Finally, we're moving into a village. I hope we didn't forget anything. What will it be like to live in the mountains with no electricity or running water?

Just like the other times we had visited, the trail was lined with people when we entered the village. A vehicle entering this remote community was obviously a big event and everyone seemed to stop what they were doing to see who was coming. Our little convoy pulled up under our new home that Scott had been building for the past three months. Though work still needed to be done, the house was ready enough to move in. What was left could be finished while we lived in it.

As we climbed out of our truck, many villagers offered to carry our belongings inside. Harry, Audrey and their boys had moved up a week before us. Like the rest of the village, they heard us coming and soon arrived to help.

My mind was filled with questions for Audrey…

— *How was your first week here?*
— *What is it like?*
— *How did the cooking go?*
— *Did you get swamped with people in your house?*

We placed boxes and barrels in the general area where we wanted the contents and then began opening them to put things away. However, we quickly decided to wait until later to finish. The front part of the house that enclosed the kitchen was quickly filling with people. Everyone seemed to be talking at once while watching our every move. Then they began going through our boxes. People walked through the doorway that led to our private living quarters—the living room, bedrooms and bathroom. We had no inside doors, so we slid the stove into the doorway to deter people. However, some were still bold enough to squeeze past and examine all of our belongings.

I couldn't understand what they were saying, but I was sure they were discussing the amount of stuff we had, probably wondering what some of it was. We realized that what we thought were just the necessities were things the Pwo Karen had never seen before. As I watched them examine our goods, I could almost hear Addie say again: "Nothing is private, nothing is off-limits. They will go through your cupboards and ask you for your things." We had just begun to experience how true that was.

We're Here!

Evening came quickly, so we walked across the village to the Beards' house. While Audrey fixed us a wonderful dinner, I asked her all of the questions that were on my mind earlier. We talked some, and she shared her first week's experiences with me.

We headed home as it began to get dark, but what we experienced was not the same darkness we were used to. Nighttime in the village was black and void of street lights or house lights. With two flashlights lighting the way, we walked slowly in single file along the narrow, uneven path. Daniel and Joel held our hands and Scott carried Seth as we made our way back to our new home. Once inside, Scott lit the kerosene lamps and we quickly put sheets and blankets on the boys' beds, strung up their mosquito nets and tucked them in.

Our temporary bed was a mattress on the floor and our only light was from a kerosene lamp. After blowing out the flame we settled into our bed. The air in the mountains was pleasantly cool for this time of year, and without electricity we were thankful for the gentle breeze that came through the house. Scott wrapped his arms around me and whispered a prayer of thanksgiving. *"Thank you for bringing us here, God. Bless our attempts to represent You here in this place for Your glory."* Then, tired and exhausted from the day's work, we quickly drifted off to sleep.

Before dawn the next morning, we were awakened by the sound of roosters and the villagers preparing for a new day. We could hear the steady creak, thump, creak, thump of wooden rice pounders used for cracking the hull off the rice kernels, as well as the sound of somebody splitting kindling for their cooking fire. As the sun began filling the village with light, the jingle of cow bells on the trail below our house and the chatter of people talking as they walked out of the village drew us from our sleepy haze.

I made breakfast for the five of us, but before we sat down to eat, someone called from out side. "Hey, Mung Jo," meaning Uncle, which is the polite way of addressing an older man, "do you have *ta thee*" (medicine) the man called out. Scott knew enough of the language to understand so he helped him with what he could. The medicines we had available were simple pain relievers, cough syrup, vitamins and cold medicine.

On Display

Before we were able to eat breakfast, the house filled with observers just like the day before. We were clearly the most exciting show in the area. We must have looked strange to them as we sat on our chairs. So that our kids could sit at the table and reach their food, they sat on stools while our youngest was strapped into a high chair so he wouldn't fall out. I'm sure they thought it would have been much easier to put the food on the floor so everyone could reach it without the use of stools and chairs. Nevertheless, we ate our breakfast feeling like a display in a storefront window.

We found no relief from the constant onlookers as there were people hanging around watching us the entire day. Putting the boys down for their naps was not easy with all the people in the house. Some even wanted to come in and find out what I was doing that took so long in the back bedrooms. Addie had been right when she warned Audrey and me to be "mentally prepared" because "curious eyes" would watch every move we made.

I had no idea how challenging this would be and wondered if I was prepared for it. Not being able to understand what they were-saying made it more difficult... Maybe it was better that I couldn't.

The villager's looks made me feel nervous and insecure. My imagination ran wild: *"Were they laughing at me? What were they saying?"* However, prepared or not, nosey villagers hung around for many days until the novelty of our presence finally began to wear off.

Making our House a Home

The very first morning we were in the village, Scott began finishing projects around the house. Inside doors were the first priority—especially one for the bathroom! Some of the men who had helped him build the house were available to help, so within a week the house was more livable for us.

After hanging the doors, Scott put shelves in the pantry for the large quantity of food and supplies we would need to store there. Then he made a bed frame for our mattress, and because we hadn't brought dressers, he built shelves for our clothes. Later we discovered that bugs make their homes in the wood, which meant we had to shake piles of wood dust off of our clothes before wearing them.

Scott put shutters on the windows to keep the bugs out at night and to prevent little Karen eyes from watching us during our meals! Fortunately, since our house was built on a slope and one side was high off the ground, we didn't have to worry about kids gawking at us from that side.

With no modern luxuries, my household duties started to consume all of my time. I had no washing machine, so clothes had to be washed by hand daily or I would get behind. Every morning after breakfast I took our basket of laundry along with the laundry tubs, detergent and a scrub brush down the hill to a water spigot not too far from our house. There, on a wooden platform, I squatted and washed, scrubbed and wrung out our laundry.

When Scott was away, Seth, our youngest, was strapped to my back as I washed our clothes. It was exhausting, taking an hour or more each time, plus hanging them up to dry. True frustration set in when during the rainy season, our clothes would take three days to dry and then smell like mildew when we wore them. Even greater frustration occurred when the clean, wet laundry tipped over and was covered with powdery red dirt so that I had to start over again!

Disposable diapers were not an option as they were a pricey new luxury in Thailand that created big disposal problems. Therefore, since Seth was in diapers day and night and Joel still wore them at night, cloth diapers alone made for lots of laundry. Jeans, sheets and blankets were the hardest to do. By the time the laundry was finished each day my hands hurt from wringing the clothes before hanging them on clotheslines to dry. Most of the morning was gone by the time I was finished, then it was time to put the boys down for a nap, lunch needed to be prepared, and the breakfast dishes had to be put away.

Adjusting to our New Life

Throughout the day, people came for medicine, so Scott and I worked together to meet what needs we could. Scott had a head start on the language so he helped me learn how to give simple instructions such as, "Take two tablets three times a day."

Cooking was a challenge as well. I was accustomed to cooking on a gas stove, but using only canned meat made many dishes very unappetizing. For instance, Thai stir fry dishes tasted okay, but the meat turned to mush as I tried to fry it. I ended up with clumpy gravy that had vegetables swimming around in it.

We had a small camper refrigerator with a freezer the size of a shoe box, so things like butter were a luxury. Instead I used a yellow, shortening-like substance that is popular in Thailand and does not require refrigeration. I wish I could say it was butter flavored, but "plastic" would be a more accurate description. The shelf-life after opening must be at least twelve years. I had a partial tub of it in the village for years, and it never changed a bit.

The first several months were very hard on Scott and me as we struggled to communicate with the people and understand the culture. Our three young boys adjusted quickly and thrived in village life. They weren't shy and started to play with the Karen children right away. Before we knew it, they quit using Thai and were speaking Karen. By the time Seth began to speak, he used as much Karen as English. He quickly became so popular around the older village kids, that they carried him everywhere. Seth was fed everywhere he went, often coming home with a fat, dirty little fist full of sweet potato, corn or bamboo shoots.

As our team adjusted to the living conditions we all began making friends and learning the language, all with the hope of telling people about God and His plan of salvation. We continued to pray that God would cultivate open hearts—people who were prepared to hear the message and embrace it. However, it was evident that for now they were steeped in spiritual bondage and fear which lead to physical pain, suffering and needless death.

Chapter 5

Spiritual Strongholds

Our simple wooden house stood very near the top of the village, which sprawled across the side of the mountain. One side of the house faced the valley that we traveled through on our way up to the village. The ground on that side was steep and quickly dropped away. Only the rooftops of the houses below us were visible, as bushes, trees and bamboo filled the spaces in between. Farther down the hill, foliage hid the houses entirely. Big clusters of bamboo stalks lazily bended as the tops swayed back and forth in the wind. Down the valley, clearings for fields and groups of houses looked very tiny. Mountains and hills on all sides of the valley framed it in.

Nearby on a different mountainside we could see the Karen village of Klompae where Bobbie and Addie had lived. It was a reminder to us of a place where the people had rejected the Word of God not many years before. The missionaries had done all the right things—they had learned the language, built friendships and taught the Bible—but the people were not ready to receive. Thus they were left, for now, in a state of spiritual darkness. Seeds had no doubt been planted, and our prayer was that God would continue to work in their hearts until they desired to know the truth.

My Place of Solitude

Our porch overlooked the valley and was a place of solitude for me, away from the bustle of village life and curious eyes of villagers. I loved reading my Bible there. Sometimes I would sit on the porch and pray while the boys slept, and would sense the Holy Spirit reassuring me to continue trusting God to do great things in this tribe for His glory.

With this awesome view to enjoy everyday, we soaked in God's wonderful creation. We enjoyed beautiful rainbows, distant lightning storms, colorful sunsets and brilliant starry nights. We heard the clacking of the wooden bells on water buffalo and the tinkling of metal cow bells as the animals were herded to and from pasture.

I planted lemon grass, cilantro, basil and peppers in wooden boxes on the porch as well as some flowers and a few tomato plants. When I was tired of the villagers watching my every move, I could look out the window at my kitchen sink and enjoy the great view of my herb garden, the valley and the lush mountains beyond.

Difficult to Understand

With no running water or electricity, the remote and primitive lifestyle was challenging at times. However, we struggled even more when it came to understanding the Karen culture and way of thinking. We had many eye-opening experiences during our initial weeks there, but even after we had been in Maepae for years, we still came across situations that left us puzzled and wondering how these people could believe such absurd things.

Our first encounter with spiritual strongholds among the Karen came during the first few weeks we were there. Our beautiful view of the valley was somewhat obstructed by an old, ugly dead tree that towered thirty feet in the air near our porch. Scott went to one of our neighbors and said, "I would like to cut that tree down, it's old and dead, and it blocks the view."

"It is a sacred tree and cannot be cut down. Years ago we used this tree to hang placentas on," the man explained. "Doing this insures the health of the newborn babies."

The ugly tree had spiritual significance and could not be cut down! As it towered before us, it was a daily reminder of the spiritual bondage the people lived in. It was ugly and had no life or hope of life in its trunk, yet we could not get rid of it.

The only bit of life on the tree did not come from any life remaining inside the tree itself, but instead a small parasitic plant about a foot tall was growing from the top of it. A seed had been dropped on the top of the tree and had sprouted. It was almost as if the Lord was using this plant to show us a picture of our little family and our team: *You have brought hope and life for My glory to this big village controlled by Satan and the forces of darkness.*

We Will Help

We hoped that one day we could speak Karen well enough to share the good news of Jesus Christ, but until then we could only offer assistance for some of their physical needs. To facilitate that, we kept a limited supply of medicine and first aid materials on hand, and offered free transportation to the hospital for those in need of more extensive help. Nevertheless, our help was not always accepted. Sometimes the person chose to remain in pain or in a life threatening condition rather than receive the free help we offered. Someday they would have a choice about their spiritual condition as well, and we hoped their choice would be freedom in Christ.

One day a sudden commotion erupted near a neighbor's house. A child was screaming uncontrollably, and people were gathering out front. Scott and I rushed down to see what had happened and if we could help.

Our neighbor lady, Taaboi, was holding her son, trying to calm him. His face was bloody, especially around the mouth. "What happened?" Scott asked.

"He fell off the porch," she answered.

As Scott and I checked him over, we could see that he had put his bottom row of teeth through his lower lip leaving a large gash. The wound was packed with dirt and bleeding badly.

"I can take you and your son to a clinic in town and get him stitched up," Scott said to the boy's father who was standing nearby.

"No, no, no, I don't have any money," the father responded.

"I will pay for it,"

"No, it won't be fun," the father said.

Fun? Whoever said we were doing this because it was fun? I thought.

Scott pleaded with him, "Listen, I'll take your son, pay for it all and bring him back. You don't even have to go." But our neighbor still showed no interest.

"No, he's alright," he said. After more pleading, he still refused.

Scott and I walked away very frustrated. We saw the need and wanted to help, but couldn't do anything about it. The boy's mouth and lip did eventually heal and only a scar remained, but their reasoning made no sense to us. This would not be the last medical argument we would have with the Karen people. For some, the battle would be between life and death.

Frail Little Byte

One day while walking by a small hut not far from our house, I heard a child whimpering inside. I stopped to chat with the mom who was outside splitting wood for cooking the evening meal. Though my language ability was still very limited, I wanted to understand what was wrong with the child by using what language I knew and listening for words that were familiar to me. Fortunately, while we were still trying to communicate, her husband returned from the fields and joined us. He could speak a little Thai, so I was able to ask him about his sick child.

"Oh, Byte has been sick for quite a while now," he said. "We will be doing a spirit ceremony for her tonight."

"What sickness does she have?" I asked.

"Rice doesn't taste good to her. She doesn't eat much. She is weak, and has diarrhea," he explained.

"Can I go in and look at her?" I inquired.

After giving his permission, the mom led me up the ladder into the house. The scene that unfolded before my eyes was heartbreaking. The small girl was lying in a dirty hammock in the dark dingy hut all by herself. Byte was hardly older than a year and very frail. She lay there motionless except for her eyes, which opened from time to time. I couldn't tell if she was even aware of our presence.

Little Byte kept moaning and seemed too weak to even cry. Her arms and legs were thin, but her belly protruded from under her little shirt. I knew she had a younger sister who was no more than a month old, which probably meant that her mother had to wean Byte suddenly, resulting in malnutrition. I had no means to deal with something this severe and felt overwhelmed with pity for her, but her parents didn't seem that concerned.

I quickly went home so I could tell Scott about this child, wondering why they had not come to us or taken her to the doctor before now.

"Honey, Byte is really sick. She needs to be taken to the hospital."

"Well, let's see if they will go," Scott said, so the two of us walked back down the hill to talk to the parents again.

To our relief, we were able to convince them to take her to the doctor. Scott drove them down the mountains and into town where she was immediately admitted to the hospital. The unfamiliar surroundings turned out to be more uncomfortable for the father than he had expected. After only two days, he had had enough and returned home with his, still very sick little daughter. He had left the hospital without the doctor's permission, so he didn't get any medication for her. When he explained why he had come back, he sounded just like our neighbor a few weeks earlier.

"It wasn't fun at the hospital, she was not getting better, and all she did was cry," he said. "I came back to do another spirit ceremony."

Less than a week later little Byte died in her father's arms while on the way to another spirit ceremony in Klompae. We were devastated when we heard the news. I felt so bad, wondering if we had done enough. Maybe we hadn't said enough, maybe we could have done more, but in the end they made a choice. They decided to depend upon the spirits to heal her. Just like the people in Klompae who years before had had the chance to hear about God's free gift of salvation through Bobbie and Addie, but did not see the need and were not ready to receive it. It is terribly sad to see people so bound by Satan that they risk the lives of their children.

Spirit Worship and Nutrition

As Scott and I talked, he reminded me that all we can do is offer our help...the decision is theirs. We cannot take on guilt for what happened. We did what we could. They could choose to live in bondage to their traditions and beliefs, or they could accept a new way of thinking and allow us to help them at no cost.

I couldn't help but be reminded of God's free gift of salvation for all who believe. One day we would be able to tell them the truth about God and His love freely offered. Then they would either accept or reject that truth.

We faced this kind of aggravation more than once in the years we lived there. Sometimes we were able to help, but other times the villagers refused. Byte was not the only one who died as a result of relatives taking too much time to appease the spirits instead of going for medical help. At times, like Byte's father, some appeared more concerned about their own comfort than their sick child. We felt helpless watching people make these kinds of decisions, especially when it had fatal effects on children.

Scott and I realized through these situations that our well-intended help could not bring about transformation in their hearts. They did not believe that modern medical help could deliver them, so they did not accept it when it was freely offered to them. Likewise we knew that unless they saw their need for God to save them from eternal punishment, they would reject it. They needed God to produce in them a desire to know Him and discontentment with the ability of the spirits to protect them.

The hold of the spirits on the people often kept from them the very thing that would do them the most good. Children battling malnutrition was common and most of them lacked the proper protein found in meat, eggs and beans. Meat and eggs were only consumed in very small quantities because they were saved for spirit ceremonies. We discovered that a small red bean that was native to the area was very high in protein. We began growing this bean ourselves to give to families who had malnourished children, and we also encouraged them to plant their own. One man explained that he could not take any to plant because this bean is called the "orphan bean." He said that if he planted the bean, his parents would die and he would become an orphan.

We had not realized the significant relationship between spirit worship and nutrition, but soon discovered that it did not end there. One of our neighbors, Chaa Duay, told Scott one day that we must destroy our garden. "It is causing problems in my family and I need you to get rid of it." He said.

Our garden was situated between our two houses and he claimed that it was affecting him. Chaa Duay had recently been to our house for medicine for his son. We had given him vitamins and cold medicine on credit since he said he did not have any money. He had been giving the medicine to his son for two days and the child was not better. Chaa Duay then divined with the spirits and they told him that he needed to get rid of his garden near his house. He thought that since our garden was close by, he should ask us to tear ours out as well just to be sure. His son was already lacking proper nutrition and now he was told to tear out his garden!

We didn't want to lose our garden or see Chaa Duay destroy food that was good for his son, so Scott asked if he would change his mind. Scott told him that if he kept his garden, and let us keep ours, he wouldn't have to pay us back for the medicine we gave him. Scott told him that his son needs better food to be healthy and that what was growing in his garden was good for him to eat.

Chaa Duay thought about it for a moment, and then agreed that we could both keep our gardens. With the help of vitamins and good food, his son recovered from his chronic cold and returned to good health.

The Power of Sorcery

Another time, wailing pierced the air in the village, and like everyone else, I stopped what I was doing and listened for the direction from which it came. Chills ran over me, because I knew that another soul had perished without knowing Christ. I could easily guess that it was Mang Gle who died. He had been sick for a month or more and was said to have been the victim of sorcery. The family had refused our offer of medical help for they said that only the spirits could save him from the curse.

It all started several months before when he and Luu Jee had a dispute. After disagreeing sharply, they parted ways. Several nights later Mang Gle dreamed that Luu Jee handed him a piece of meat, which he took and then ate. When he awakened, he remembered the dream and fearfully realized his doom. He wasted no time in telling his friends and family about the dream. They all tried to console him for they all knew that particular dream was a sure sign of sorcery.

As the news spread in the village fear gripped everyone, especially Luu Jee, the man who is said to have performed the sorcery. He wasted no time leaving the village because he knew that this would lead to his murder whether he was guilty or not. Sorcerers were quickly assassinated because everyone feared their destructive power. He knew that he may only have days until Mang Gle became ill, proving the success of the spell. He also knew that he had not cast a spell, but as soon as sickness came no one would believe him. Luu Jee took what he could and moved out of the mountains to a town near Maesariang where he would have the protection of civilization and the police.

When sorcery is successful, it is said that a cow's liver is implanted in the abdomen of the victim. By eating the meat in the dream, the cow's liver gets inside the body and begins killing its victim. Only about a week after his dream, Mang Gle began suffering from stomach pain. Every ceremony his family tried was unsuccessful. As he continued to decline, the entire village knew his fate. Soon he would join the "village of the dead."

When a person dies, the custom in Pwo Karen culture is to wrap the body in a woven mat. Then they are either laid in the house if the house will be destroyed after the funeral. If not in the house, they are laid on a table of bamboo poles with a small roof over it that is erected just outside the house. The body remains there for the duration of the funeral, usually lasting 3-5 days.

When the day of Mang Gle's burial finally came, Scott and Barry were told that this funeral would be different from the others they had seen, so they decided to observe. Friends and family were gathered around the house and there were a few men who were preparing to transport the body to the burial grounds. Scott and Barry watched from a little distance as the men worked. When the breeze blew their direction, the stench that came from the body was nauseating as it had been laying there for five days by this time.

A sturdy bamboo pole was placed on top of the mat that contained the body. The pole extended beyond the head and feet by several feet. The men slightly lifted one end of the mat to pass a rope under it and securely fastened it to the carrying pole. They did this at each end then passed a couple of ropes under the middle of the body. They lifted up on the pole already fastened to one end to create enough space under the body to pass the ropes. Scott and Barry were again hit with the stench as they observed that the underside of the mat was wet from the decaying body.

When all the ropes were secured and other preparations were completed, the men of the village began the procession carrying the body inside the cocoon of the woven mat out to the burial grounds.

Traditionally the Karen people bury their dead in shallow graves but this would be unlike the usual ceremony.

I looked down on the trail from our porch and saw that only men were going, and many of them were carrying belongings of the deceased. Some carried clothes, others knives, his black powder rifle and some of his tools were also taken with him. A few people carried food on a tiny tray made from banana leaves and bamboo.

When the group reached the burial grounds many different things took place all at once. Some of the men began destroying the man's belongings. The knives, tools and gun were bent and handles broken, his clothes were ripped and everything was hung in the trees around the area. These broken things can be used in the "crazy village" and this allows the spirit of the dead to carry these things along to the afterlife. Even the head of a cow was hung in a tree so the man could have cattle there.

Meanwhile others gathered wood. This would be a cremation instead of a burial because sorcery was the cause of death and the body must be completely destroyed. Some of the men were drinking rice whiskey and singing chants in a group around a woven tray that had symbols drawn on it. One man used a stick and pointed to the different symbols as they chanted.

Next, a few men unwrapped the body. When they had sufficiently exposed the decaying body, one man cut into the abdomen with a knife. Then one man reached inside as if searching for something. Finally he pulled out what they were looking for, the "cow's liver" which was the cause of death. They said that this "mass" was not a normal part of a human body and that it was what had caused the swelling in the abdomen. To Scott and Barry's horror, a small piece was cut off and handed to Mang Gle's brother, who, with hands trembling, took it and dropped it into his mouth, quickly washing it down with a full shot of whiskey.

As the funeral proceeded, the body was laid on the pile of wood and a fire was started. The group stayed until they were sure that everything was completely burned, making double sure that the growth in the stomach was nowhere to be found in the ashes. While they waited, Scott asked why the brother had done what he did. He was told that the Karen believe this will protect him from ever having that kind of sorcery committed on him.

When the cremation was over, the group made their way back to the village. They hurried along, because no one wanted to be at the back of the group with their back to the burial ground in case a spirit should try to catch them. As they entered the edge of the village just below our house, there was a bucket of water sitting on the trail with a bundle of white cotton string draped over the edge. As each one came to the bucket, he squatted down and washed his hands, then took two pieces of string and tied one to each wrist.

Scott and I talked that evening about the events of the day and the incredible grip the spirits had upon the people. We took hope in the promise of Jesus himself as He told those who were listening, *"If you hold to my teaching, you are really my disciples. Then you will know the truth and the truth will set you free"* (John 8:31-32 NIV). Then we prayed for the Karen people to one day accept the freedom that could be theirs through the truth of the gospel, the message of grace and the love of God.

Chapter 6

God Paves the Way

While we were still living in the town of Maesariang, surveying and deciding which village our team should move into, Scott went to visit some friends who were Baptist missionaries. These missionaries were working on translation and heading up a literacy program for the Pwo Karen. They had developed literacy books and teacher's guides and conducted teacher training classes. They also ran a dorm for Pwo Karen children from the mountain villages who wanted to continue their education beyond what was offered in their own schools. At the time the Thai government only offered education through fourth grade in remote areas. If children wanted to continue studying, they had to stay at a dorm in a larger town and attend school there.

Several years earlier, a young man from Maepae named Not Tu lived in the Baptist dorm and was able to complete an eighth grade education. While there, he was also exposed to Christian beliefs by attending church where he learned to sing hymns and pray. He also learned to read in his own language and excitedly read any story given to him. He was given several booklets containing stories from the Bible; some were from the Old Testament and others were from the gospels. Not Tu was so interested in reading these stories that in the evenings when the missionaries taught from God's Word, he would sit in the back and read his booklets. Therefore, he did not understand the spiritual truths in them because he was not listening to the teaching, but just reading the stories as if they were fiction.

Improving Language Skills

When Not Tu was around 19 years old, he returned to Maesariang. He and a couple other young men from Maepae had heard that the missionaries there were hiring men to teach literacy in the mountain villages. Because he could use the money and liked to read he decided to give it a try.

The day Scott and Not Tu met, Scott told him we would be moving to Maepae to teach God's Word and he appeared very interested. By this time, Not Tu had been teaching literacy for two years in some mountain villages. One day after teaching literacy in the village of Klompae, he sat with some young men who were listening to a story about God on a hand-crank tape player the Storey's had left. The younger men of the village were very interested in the stories and listened to them in the evenings around the fire. When the older men learned that they were listening to stories about a creator God, they warned them that the legendary giant monster, *Pii Dongkay,* would eat them as punishment. Undeterred, the young men continued to listen, but were careful to do so in secret.

Most villagers could not speak Central Thai, the national language, but Not Tu was an exception. His command of Central Thai was very good and a huge help to Scott when he was building our house as that was the language we had learned in Bangkok. Communication was a challenge as Scott worked with the villagers, but Not Tu was always willing to help. He even offered to work with

Scott and teach him the language once we moved in, so Scott hired him to be his language helper.

Not Tu had become an excellent reader and writer of his own language, thereby making him a tremendous asset. Scott could talk with the people, write down what he heard, and then bring it back to Not Tu for correction. This guaranteed that Scott learned every new word and phrase with an accurate spelling and pronunciation. This was such a miracle.

From Bother to Blessing

We were overjoyed with God's faithfulness and were awestruck with how He had provided someone so fit for the job. We prayed for prepared hearts and God had answered above and beyond all we could have asked or thought. Nevertheless, with a mountain of language and culture study to do, the reality of a mature and functioning church seemed like a distant hope. But God was preparing Not Tu to be more than just a language helper.

Often God's hand in preparing the way for us was not obvious. Many days I longed for peace and quiet because the Karen villagers were in our house nearly every day. I complained to God often about this until the day Scott encouraged me with the fact that God was using their constant presence to familiarize me with the Karen language. I didn't even have to leave the house! They came to our house for medicine and first aid, which enabled us to earn their trust and begin building a rapport. I realized that Scott was right and that I was truly beginning to understand their language and build friendships! After I realized what God was doing, their constant presence became much more of a blessing to me.

However, God didn't stop there. He knew all of our needs. One of my greatest needs was quickly becoming a physical one. We had moved into the village with three little boys, no electricity, no running water and no washing machine. We had no convenience foods like packaged mixes, store-bought bread or pizza delivery. This meant that my days were filled with laundry, making meals, caring for the boys and the house, medical work, as well as trying to fit in some language learning time.

One day while I was doing laundry, my hands tired from scrubbing and wringing out clothes, Not Tu came up the path. The morning had almost completely passed consumed by nothing but my daily chores. He stopped and watched me for a minute and then said that his brother's wife needed work and he wondered if I would be willing to hire her to do laundry. He told me that her name was Chuu Gee, that her husband was in jail, and that she was trying to support her children by herself.

I was very grateful for this opportunity and knew that it was yet another provision from God. With a big smile on my face, I told Not Tu that I would like to have her come and work for us but needed to talk with Scott about it first.

God Sends a Friend

Just a few days later, Chuu Gee started to work for us. She was about 37 years old but looked much older from the hard life she lived. Like the other women, she wore beads and bangles around her neck and brass bracelets all the way up her arms. Her long black hair was done in typical Karen style, pulled forward from the back into a ponytail at the top of her forehead and then laid back across the top of the head and down the back, secured with silver clips. She wore a hand-woven red shirt and skirt like all of the married women did. Chuu Gee had high, prominent cheek bones, typical of the Karen people, and teeth stained reddish black from chewing a native concoction wrapped in a leaf. Her eyes, however, were very friendly.

Chuu Gee had been working at a mica mine three kilometers down the mountain. She walked there and back every day for a wage of just two dollars a day. To work there meant leaving her baby in the village to be cared for by her other children who were only four and seven at the time. However, now that she worked for us, she could stay in the village and look after her youngest child while she worked.

Chuu Gee was kind and very patient with me and the kids. She could not speak Thai, so for a long time we communicated with hand gestures. She also taught me practical Karen words when people came to the house and I needed to communicate something. She was with me almost all day every day, and soon seemed to know what I was thinking and would even create sentences for me and help me say them correctly. She was not only my house helper, but also my unofficial language tutor. More importantly, she became my closest friend.

Once again, we saw God faithfully at work paving the way for us. There were many times God gave us wisdom beyond our years and would lead us on the spot to be able to help people in need.

Chapter 7

Learning as We Go

Evenings were very peaceful. The usual busyness of the day had died down and the only noises were from crickets and a few other night creatures. The air was cool bringing relief from the heat of the day, and no one else was in our house except our family.

One evening after the boys were in bed, Scott and I sat in the living room talking by the soft light of a kerosene lantern. I was relieved we would soon go to bed as Scott and I were both tired from a busy day.

New Adventures

Suddenly our dog began to bark and the serenity of the moment was shattered. We hadn't heard anyone come up to the house, but a moment later heard the voice of a man calling Scott's name. We hushed the dog and Scott answered back with the common *"huh"* of acknowledgement.

"Are you sleeping?" the man asked.

We both got up to open the front door and a Karen man entered the house, blowing out the flaming pieces of pine pitch he had used to light his way.

"Can you come and look at my wife?" He asked us, "Her stomach hurts."

"Where is she?" Scott asked.

"She is at home, on the other side of the village. Come and see if the baby is ready to be born."

Scott turned to me and asked if I wanted to go check her out.

"Sure. I'll go see what I can do." I replied.

I went back to the bedroom to get a flashlight. On my way back to the kitchen at the front of the house, Scott met me and gave me a hug. Then he said, "I'll pray for you. God will give you wisdom."

"Thank you, Honey. I love you."

"Love you, too," he replied.

My quiet evening was quickly turning into an entirely new adventure. Shining the light for both of us, I followed the man as we walked toward his home. Though I was tired, a sudden burst of energy surged through me. Childbirth was a part of Karen culture that I had wondered about, and now I was going to witness it firsthand.

Primitive Birthing

I had no idea what to do if any complications arose and hoped all would go well. Though this couple thought I was going to help, my intention was to simply observe. However, if a problem was encountered, Scott would take her to the hospital if they were willing.

I followed the man along a dark, narrow footpath, which was the back way to the other side of the village. With very little light he moved along with ease in his flip-flops as if he knew every step of the way. I did my best to shine the light a little in front of him so he could see while not leaving myself totally in the dark. The path was no more than a foot wide, and in places completely covered with leaves that hid small roots and uneven ground. Nevertheless, I walked as fast as I could, being careful to keep my balance.

Finally we came to the end of the small trail on the other side of the village. After passing only a few houses, we crossed the main trail and walked up to a small bamboo house. Like all the others in the village, this one had a thatched roof and a short ladder reaching from the porch to the ground. The man quickly climbed the ladder and removed his flip-flops. I followed him, but not quite as nimbly. The ladder's rungs were round and my feet were unsteady on them so I held the edge of the porch to steady myself as I went up. Dim light from the small fire inside was visible through the doorway. I stooped to enter the house and felt the split bamboo floor give under my weight as I walked across the tiny house.

The man's wife was on the other side of the fire box, her belly protruding like a basketball tucked under her skirt. A small fire was burning, which filled the room with smoke. She was sitting on her heels with her knees on the floor. Her hands were stretched above her head and she held tightly to an old hand-woven shirt. The shirt was tied to the ends of a rope that hung from the bamboo rafters of the hut. Her position looked very uncomfortable and tiring.

The woman's husband quickly moved in behind her, squatted on the floor and placed his knees against the small of her back. As contractions came, she pulled on the rope and leaned back to straighten her torso. Her husband reached around her stomach, locked his fingers and squeezed at the top of her belly. She made a quiet groaning sound at the peak of the pain. When the contraction was over, she relaxed a bit, but his grip on her upper abdomen stayed steady as if to force the baby out with pressure.

I felt terribly sorry for this woman! I wouldn't want anyone squeezing on my belly during delivery.

I sat down on the floor beside the woman and whispered a prayer, *"Lord, please show me what to do."* I had no medical training, but having three of my own children I knew that timing the contractions would reveal about how far along she was. I slipped off my watch, put it in my lap and then turned on the flashlight. Then I positioned my free hand on her stomach and waited for another contraction. It took a few contractions for me to remember how to time them, but soon figured it out and decided that she was very close to delivery.

As the minutes passed, I continued timing contractions, but became aware that the couple was waiting for my diagnosis. Then the man asked, "What time will the baby be born? How much longer will it be?" I realized this couple thought I could tell by looking at my watch when the baby would come. I told them I was not sure, but thought that it would not be too much longer.

After thirty minutes or so, the woman said she had to urinate and then slowly stood and waddled out of the house onto the porch. As we waited, I again asked the Lord for wisdom and an uncomplicated delivery. Then, just as the woman returned to the doorway, a sudden gush of water splashed her bare feet. She stopped momentarily to wait for a contraction to end and then carefully walked across the floor to resume her former position with her husband behind her.

I checked her progress again, this time under her skirt, and could see the baby's head beginning to show. I knew then it wouldn't be long until the baby came.

A New Little Life

During the next few contractions, she pushed hard along with the help of her husband. With her husband behind her, no one but me was in a position to catch the baby. I wondered what they would have done had I not been there. Though it would have been a short fall, the landing would have been head-first.

"It's a girl," I announced. Being very wet and wiggly, she was very hard to hold.

Even though I had three boys of my own, I had experienced nothing like the miracle of life born before my eyes. *"Thank-you, Lord for this little life."*

The baby's dark hair was wet and matted against her head. Her little face was beautiful and perfectly formed. She cried a good healthy cry as all of her senses were shocked with the sudden change of environment. A few moments later, the placenta came, and I knew the cord must be cut. I was unfamiliar with all the necessary precautions and was afraid I wouldn't do it right, so I sat holding the baby and watched.

The new father stood and pulled two strings off of the edge of a woven bag that was draped over a bamboo pole stretched across a corner of the room. Then he snapped a thin piece of bamboo off the wall. He came over to the baby and tied the dirty strings in two places on the umbilical cord near her belly. Then, using the rock as a cutting board under the cord between the strings, he used the bamboo fragment as a knife to cut the cord. After cutting the cord, he used his regular knife to cut a short length of bamboo. Using the bamboo as a tube, he cut off one end just under one of the ridges so it would have a solid bottom leaving the top end open like a vase.

I had asked for warm water to wash the baby, but was given a small tub of cold water instead. The bath caused the tiny girl to exercise her healthy lungs once again as she was doused with cold water. I didn't want to chill her, so I used a rag the father gave me to dry her and another one to wrap her in. Then I held her tight to comfort and warm her.

What Next?

The father used the bamboo tube he had prepared to hold the placenta. Then he draped an old piece of a shirt over it and fastened with a thin piece of bamboo wrapped twice around the top of the cylinder. Pulling it tight, he twisted the two ends together like a twist tie and then set it aside to bury later. He helped his wife slide closer to the fire and then poured water onto the floor where the blood was, rubbing it with his foot. The bloody water flowed through the cracks in the floor and splashed on the ground below where the pigs slept.

I noticed that the mother seemed disinterested in the baby. I was unsure if she was unhappy or fearful, but she made no move to hold her new little girl. When I held the baby close so she could look at her precious little face, the mother's expression did not change; she just glanced at her baby and then turned away.

The mother motioned for me to lay the newborn on the floor a little ways from herself. Though she could not reach the baby from there, I did as she told me and laid her on the floor wrapped in dirty rags. The father went outside and brought in two bamboo poles about three feet long. He used these to make a backrest for his wife against the frame of the drying rack at the edge of the fire box. When he was finished, he helped her scoot back to lean against them. He then stoked the fire and asked if she was warm enough. She softly replied that she was, but seemed afraid to move more than her eyes and lips. She held her head very still and sat on the floor, legs extended in front of her, leaning back by the fire.

The father rummaged around in a corner for a moment and came back to the fire with another piece of old clothing in his hand. Using the cloth he draped it over a flat, saucer-sized smooth stone that was lying in the ashes near the fire. He wrapped the hot stone in the rag and gave it to his wife. She took it and with both hands pressed it against her lower abdomen. The warmth must have felt good as she seemed to relax some.

By this time the baby had kicked off her covering and had started to cry. Mom glanced over, but made no move to comfort her little one. I picked up the baby and tried wrapping her again, but the rag was rough and hardly big enough to cover her.

As I cuddled the baby and looked at her sweet little face, it seemed unfortunate that she was born here in this dirty little hut, breathing smoky air and wrapped in nothing but rags. She is, however, one of millions of children born into similar conditions all over the world. Even Jesus, Son of the Almighty God, was born in such surroundings, if not worse. He came to serve, not to be served, and to seek and save that which was lost. He did not come in splendor or comfort as a king, but as a carpenter's son in a shelter for animals.

More of God's Plan Revealed

As I left the little house and walked home through the darkness, I thanked God for no complications in this birth. Both the mom and the baby seemed to be doing well. Nevertheless, I knew that I had to educate myself on childbirth in the event I was ever asked to help with another delivery.

God was preparing me for a ministry with women in an area where I had no skill or knowledge of my own. I was not a nurse and had no medical background, so I would have to depend totally upon God. Scott and I had learned over the years that dependence upon Him is the most awesome place to be. We would see God do many miraculous things among the Karen people, not because of us, but because of the power of God's mighty hand in bringing a people unto Himself.

Living in a sin-cursed world, however, means that everyone will experience sickness, sorrow and death. Therefore, we were very sad to hear that this beautiful little baby girl died just ten days after being born. Umbilical tetanus, we learned, caused many infant deaths within the first few days of life. No doubt tetanus germs were on the tools used to cut the umbilical cord resulting in an infection that ravaged her tiny body.

The infant mortality rate within the first ten days was high in the mountain villages since there were no vaccines and little concept of cleanliness. In the minds of the Karen people however, every death had a spiritual cause. Maintaining spiritual harmony was especially delicate throughout pregnancy, during birth and the few days that followed. I have witnessed a baby still attached to the umbilical cord being fed a few grains of rice to try to ensure the child's health. Taboos were much more numerous during this period and breaking them was practically inevitable. They believe their only hope depends upon detecting the offended spirit and making restitution before death occurs. In this hardened culture, infants ten days old or less are not given a normal funeral. Instead, they are quietly disposed of with no wailing or mourning.

The Karen people routinely wait for ten days before naming a child since the death rate is so high. With that knowledge it became clear to me why the mother seemed disinterested in the baby. She was protecting herself from becoming emotionally attached in the event the baby didn't survive; a grief which was all too familiar to her. This woman and her husband had experienced eight such deaths, raising only five children to maturity.

Fear for the mother's life during the fragile days of pregnancy and birth was also very real. It was customary to allow a new mother to only eat rice, salt and hot peppers for several days after the delivery. This often caused an already weak mother to regain her strength very slowly. This, coupled with the nutrients that flowed to the nursing baby, depleted the mother even more. However, fear of the spirits overpowered any cravings for vegetables, fish, eggs or fruit, which kept mothers in a very vulnerable physical state.

Nevertheless, God used these heartaches in the lives of some to cause discouragement with the cycle of sickness and loss of life. When the spirits failed them time after time, some began to look elsewhere.

Chapter 8

Prepared Hearts

The thief does not come except to steal, and to kill, and to destroy. I have come that they may have life, and that they may have it more abundantly.
John 10:10 (NKJV)

Two Karen people are animists; they worship spirits and live in fear of them. They believe that every healthy person has thirty-three personal spirits, and that as long as taboos are not broken, health and good fortune are ensured.

These people believe the spirits of the village become angry when a taboo is broken and will steal a spirit from that person or a family member as punishment. When a spirit has been taken from an individual, they believe it causes illness or tragedy of some kind.

Spirits that reign over the village can become offended in literally hundreds of ways. Some of the taboos are so petty that it's hard to know if an offense has occurred until someone in the family is sick. Even animals can bring illness or misfortune to the family. If a pig has a litter of all male or all female babies, the babies and mother must be killed in order to make atonement for the offense. Likewise, if a dog jumps over the tray of rice, misfortune is sure to follow unless the dog is killed to make amends.

Spiritual Desperation

When someone is sick, they must find out which spirit was offended and triggered the sickness, so a shaman is hired to do divination. He can use a host of different items to divine with the spirits, such as chicken bones, leaves from guava trees, rice, strips of bamboo or other items.

After the shaman tells them which spirit was offended, a ritual ceremony must be done to appease the spirit. During many of these rituals, a chicken is sacrificed, the blood drained and the meat cooked to be eaten by everyone in the family. A shaman then prays to the spirits, asking them to accept the sacrifice in return for the spirit of the person who is sick. The shaman then ties white cotton string around the wrists of each family member while he chants a blessing over them.

Many people experience hopeless frustration with spirit worship. About two years before we moved into the village, Gle La, one of Not Tu's brothers, and his wife had become disillusioned with appeasing the spirits. Unable to escape the sickness that plagued their family, they had repeatedly paid for the village shaman to divine with the spirits to reveal which one had been upset. Ceremony after ceremony had been done using all of their pigs and chickens as sacrifices. Because they had no more of their own animals, they were forced to buy more from their family and friends in the hope that the spirits would be appeased and their two young sons would get well.

None of the shaman's rituals worked. Gle La and his wife watched helplessly as both of their boys became weaker. They both died just a few months apart leaving their parents heartbroken and childless.

The Search for Truth

Feeling betrayed and defeated, Gle La and his wife began searching elsewhere for protection for the new baby that was on the way and for themselves. They talked to many people, searching for answers to their questions, though many people in the village told them they needed to keep trying more sacrifices and ceremonies. Gle La could not be convinced, however, that the old way was the best way.

When Not Tu heard about Gle La's frustration with spirit worship he explained what little he knew about Christianity and gave him one of the song books he had received at the hostel where he had lived. "People who worship God meet on Sunday mornings and sing and pray together. They listen to someone talk for a long time, and they have the 'good, white book' that tells them what to do," Not Tu explained to his brother. "God worshipers don't have to use up their animals for sacrifices. They just pray to God."

As the two talked, their oldest brother, Jo Tu, joined the conversation. He and his family had also been plagued with sickness and were ready to try something new as well.

Gle La and Jo Tu discussed the possibility of deserting their former practices and calling themselves God worshipers (Christians). Eventually, they called on a Pwo Karen pastor from a church near Maesariang to come to the village and destroy their spirit worship fetishes. He did as they asked and instructed them to meet together on Sunday mornings to sing and pray. The pastor then prayed for them and left them to worship God on their own. Shortly after, Jo Tu was arrested for selling opium and was taken to jail in Maesariang.

"Let there be Light"

This had taken place two years before our arrival in the village. During the first two months we lived there we knew nothing about the families of Gle La and Jo Tu and their interest in God.

One morning Scott came in the house with the exciting news:

> "I was just talking to Not Tu, and he told me that two of
> his brothers call themselves Christians and meet together
> on Sunday mornings with their families."

I couldn't believe my ears. When we prayed for God to prepare hearts, we never imagined anything like this.

"They want to know if we will meet with them." Scott said. "We need to tell Harry and Audrey about this."

These two families had turned from their spirit worship, but had no understanding of this new "religion." They did not know the character of God or the salvation He provided through the sacrifice of His Son, Jesus Christ. Unfortunately, we had a long way to go before we would be able to communicate any of the truths of God's Word in their language.

Jo Tu's wife, Chuu Gee, my house helper, held church in their house, even though her husband was in prison. I was overwhelmed with joy and amazement at the hand of God. Not only were there two families who were totally prepared to hear God's Word, but the lady we had hired to help with housework was one of them. God had brought us together because I had a need for help with housework, and she had a need for money to support her children. What an opportunity!

Sitting on our back porch that afternoon, I reflected on the goodness of God. Looking up at that dead tree towering in front of me, my eyes again focused on the small plant growing at the top. God had planted the seed, watered it and sprouted this plant on this lifeless tree. Much more amazing though, He had planted a seed of truth in the lives of these Pwo Karen people in the midst of spiritual emptiness. Their desire to abandon their old ways and follow God had come totally apart from our influence. Instead, God had prepared their hearts ahead of time just as we had asked. He did it; not because of our prayers, but for His glory.

Chapter 9

Death and Life

Harry, Audrey and their two boys moved into the village of Maepae a week before we did. About eight months later, Barry and Cathy Richards joined our team and began building their house in the village, which required them to make frequent trips from Maesariang to work on it.

While they were staying with us during one of their trips, a man from the village of Xwee Muu came to visit relatives in Maepae. Our house was on the edge of the village so he stopped by to tell us there had been a death in Xwee Muu that morning. A woman had been in labor most of the night with her second child. The baby was born early in the morning, but the woman was very weak and had lost a large amount of blood.

"She died this morning, after the sun came up," the man told us. "The baby is fine, but no one is able to feed her."

"What are they going to do with the baby?" I asked.

"I don't know. They may just bury her with her mom."

"Alive?"

"Yes; if no one can care for her."

When a Karen mother dies, it is taboo for a baby to be nursed by anyone other than the mother's sister...and a willing and able sister is very rare. The Karen people believe that the restless spirit of the mother will call the baby to join her in the afterlife, thus resulting in the death of the child. Adoption is considered too risky as many taboos could be broken, which would cause trouble for the adoptive family.

Adoption

Barry and Cathy had no children of their own and expressed their interest in adopting this newborn if the father would allow them to take the baby and raise her.

When Scott returned, we told him what the man had said. Scott, Barry, and a village friend named Dite Moi, took off late that afternoon to see if they could bring the baby back. They were told that the baby could not leave the village until the funeral was over, so they returned back to Maepae after dark traveling on precarious foot trails.

The next morning we decided that we had better make another trip there to take formula to the baby to keep her nourished until they would allow us to take her. This time Cathy and I wanted to go too.

At the time, no road ran directly between Maepae to Xwee Muu. Though our truck or motorcycles could go part of the way, we would have to hike the rest of the way. There was an indirect way to get there on motorcycles, but it would take a very long time.

Nevertheless, we agreed that all of us should go talk to the father about granting permission to adopt. We packed bottles and formula to take so they could keep the baby alive until the funeral ceremonies concluded. We decided to take motorbikes and go by road the long way. Scott rode one with our son, Daniel, and Dite Moi. Barry and Cathy rode on another one. Our second son, Joel, had the misfortune of riding with me. Seth was only seventeen months old so we decided to leave him in Maepae with Chuu Gee.

Off to Xwee Muu

With a few supplies packed in our bags, we headed out of the village down the rutted dirt road. The dry season had set in and it hadn't rained for a month or more so the road was thick with dust. I was thankful for the dry trail however, because my skill-level on the bike was amateur to say the least.

Twenty minutes later we were down the mountain. We drove into the Thai village in the valley and made a right turn toward the mountains in a different direction. We hadn't gone far on this new trail when I had my first spill. The road was almost entirely flat, but straw thrown down from the recent rice harvest made it slick. Suddenly the bike slid and we went down. Joel and I both fell on the soft cushion of yellow straw, but he still cried for a few minutes as we got up and gathered ourselves.

Scott jumped off his bike and ran to help us. Together we looked at Joel to make sure he was okay and saw that he had a three-inch, round hole in the shield of his helmet. Somehow Joel was not hit with the projectile and was only startled. We were so thankful that he was okay. There was no damage to the bike, so we were ready to continue.

The trail began to climb and became more narrow and rugged. The farther we went, the less traveled the road seemed. After two hours, Dite Moi told us we were getting close. Soon we saw houses and then drove into a small village.

A Grieving Family

The house where the woman had died was surrounded by people. Most of them were sitting in groups on woven mats laid out on the ground, talking, drinking or playing cards.

Dite Moi asked a man he knew where Dee Oi, the baby's father, was. He said that he had brought the *colay*, foreigners, to talk with him. The man pointed toward the small hut next door.

We were invited up into the house by a young man standing on the porch, his face burdened by grief. He couldn't have been more than twenty years old and looked too young to be the husband of the woman who had died. He still wore his hair in the style of a young single man, with a long pony tail at the side of his head that was knotted just in front of his left ear and held by silver clips.

We climbed up the ladder and ducked in through the door of the small house. Inside, three or four women squatted on the floor, all of them wiping their eyes and nose with a cloth. Each of them had unwrapped the fabric usually worn on their head and were using it as tissue.

On the floor near the wall was a woven mat folded like a cocoon around the woman's body. I wondered what she looked like thinking that she must have been very young.

A two-year-old girl toddled into the house and leaned against one of the older women squatting on the floor. The woman took her in her arms and held her close for a moment then let her go as she ran to her dad and settled into his arms. She was too little to understand what had happened to her mother.

The newborn was lying on the other side of the fire box. She was quiet and still, sound asleep. Suddenly, wailing began outside the house and quickly spread among the mourners both inside and out. This lasted only a few minutes and then gradually quieted down.

I didn't know the family, the woman, or anyone in the village, but I could feel their grief. I felt such sadness for the husband who, at such a young age, was now a widower. I felt sure that one of the older women in the house was mourning for her daughter; probably the one the child had come to.

We each found a place to sit on the floor while Dite Moi talked to Dee Oi, the man of the house. Cathy and I had sat down near the newborn baby. The baby woke up when the loud wailing began. As if joining them, she jerked awake and began to cry as well.

Cathy picked up the newborn and held her while I mixed a bottle. She was wrapped in a dirty rag and had not been cleaned up very well after birth. Everyone was more concerned about the condition of her mother after she was born. The baby had been placed on the floor while many ceremonies were performed in attempts to save the mother's life.

The spirits had seemingly won again. They had stolen a soul, taking her to a place the Karen call the crazy village of the afterlife. According to their legends, it is a place where everything is backwards.

Cathy dampened a cloth with water and cleaned the baby while I finished preparing a bottle. I handed it to Cathy and she tried to put it in the baby's mouth to feed her. The baby didn't know what to do for the first few seconds and tried to push it back out with her tongue. Then she tasted something good and quickly began sucking. She was definitely hungry as it didn't take her long to finish two ounces of formula. Cathy wrapped her in a clean blanket we had brought and held her while the men talked with her father.

"You may take her, but not today, not until we have buried her mother," he told us. "The day after tomorrow will be the burial, and then you can take the baby. I cannot care for her, so I would rather you take her."

We explained how to make bottles for the baby and how to clean everything in the hope they would do as we said. She could become very sick if they didn't follow through.

Blazing a New Trail

After about an hour, we decided to leave so we could get home before dark. We put the little baby on the floor where she had been and then headed out to the bikes.

Dite Moi, our "guide," thought it had taken too long the way we had come so he suggested we go back a different way. He informed us it was shorter and less steep...if I remember right, he said it was flat. Looking back, it seems ridiculous that we were even tempted to believe him knowing the terrain we were in.

Scott, thinking of my inexperience, asked Dite Moi if the trail was wide. Dite Moi assured him that it was. Unfortunately, we were gullible and believed him on both accounts. In blind trust, we headed out of the village in the opposite direction from where we had entered, and immediately started up a steep climb on a narrow trail about three feet wide. This was not at all what Dite Moi said it would be, but we all hoped that after this initial climb the trail would flatten out and widen.

We rode along in single file up the hill and I could tell Joel was nervous. I didn't blame him, because I was, too! His pudgy little fingers wrapped around the crossbar between the handle bars kept him in position on the tank as we climbed the hill.

We made it to the top with no problem and followed the trails that Dite Moi told us to take, sometimes taking the right fork and other times the left. The trail was flatter for a while but continued getting narrower the farther we went.

As we entered a particularly thick clump of trees, the trail was blocked by a fallen tree. We stopped our bikes and one-by-one lifted each one over the tree. Looking ahead we saw that this was not the only fallen tree in our way and had to stop and lift the bikes over four more. By now, all of us wished we hadn't listened to Dite Moi.

Steep, Rough and Narrow

Not far from all the fallen trees the trail again began to climb, but now the path was only about a foot wide. As we continued the climb, the trail shrunk to a mere six inches wide. In most places there was some room for error as both sides of the trail were edged with low weeds that could be driven through if necessary. When we were about three-quarters of the way up the hill, all room for error suddenly disappeared. The path wound around trees and over small roots with a drop-off on one side.

I became nervous and had Joel get off and ride with Scott while Dite Moi walked. As the trail crossed some larger roots at the base of a tree, I panicked and lost my balance. With the tree on the right side of me and a small drop on the other, I had no place to put my feet to catch myself. I began leaning left, but my foot didn't reach the ground so I tipped over, completely unable to prevent it. Thankfully, I had a soft landing in the thick underbrush. The bike was nearly upside down because of the slope, but I was unscathed except for a few scratches.

Dite Moi, who was already on foot, was the first to get to me and pick up the bike. Scott and the boys were scared, but soon realized I was fine. Scott started the bike for me and soon we were on our way again.

This way home was not faster. In fact the sun was setting and we didn't know how much farther we had to go. To make things worse, my arms and shoulders ached terribly from the tension of this tricky driving. Dite Moi assured us we were close, but who would believe him now? I hoped Seth was doing okay in the village this long without us.

The path became less rugged again, but the weeds and under-brush still hugged close to the trail. Cathy decided to walk in several of the more difficult spots and I caught up to her. She was about to step off to the side to let me go by when suddenly my bike jolted, and I felt intense pain in my left shin. I let off the gas and leaned over to grab my shin causing both the bike and me to fall in the brush beside the trail. As I lay holding my shin, yelling in pain, Cathy ran to me. Neither she nor I had any idea what had happened. Scott rode up behind me on the trail, unloaded the boys, and steadied his own bike on the kickstand. Then he lifted my bike and moved it out of the way.

"What happened?" he asked.

"My shin hit something back there." I said, pointing a few feet back on the trail.

"Are you okay?"

"I think so." Tears ran down my face though the pain had begun to ease. Scott went back a few feet on the trail and discovered that I had hit a stump that had been cut off at the edge of the trail. It was hidden in the underbrush, so I never saw it coming.

"Do you think you can get up?" Scott asked me. It was hurting a lot, but I knew it was not broken.

"Yeah," I said, wiping the tears from my face.

Cathy and Scott helped me up, but I couldn't put any weight on that leg. I knew that I couldn't walk home, but couldn't drive the bike home either. Scott already had the boys with him, so Barry and Cathy took one to ride with them. Scott assured me that I could ride with him and our other son. He decided to leave the bike hidden in the weeds and come back for it later. Dite Moi didn't know how to ride a bike, so he had to walk home (not that I felt sorry for him).

With Daniel sitting on the tank and me on the back, we headed for home. Every bump we hit sent pain through my leg, but I could move my foot and toes so I knew it was not broken.

We arrived just before dark and I hobbled into the house and sat down. Chuu Gee had heard us coming and brought Seth up to the house; he was very happy to see us all.

Baby Has A New Home

The day of the funeral came, and Barry and Cathy were anxious to get their little girl. We all hoped the family had taken good care of her and had done as we had told them.

After talking it over, we decided the best way to get the baby home was to carry her out on foot. The trails were too rough to manage with an infant on the motorcycle and the truck couldn't go all the way there.

Scott drove one of the motorcycles to where the truck was parked and drove it to where Barry would meet him later. Barry hiked all the way in and then several hours later returned with a cloth sling in front of him, cradling a tiny little baby. He climbed in the truck with Scott and together they returned to our house where Cathy was waiting.

Barry handed the little one to Cathy. As she looked at her she asked Barry, "So, are we going to call her Rebecca Joy?" Barry smiled and nodded his head.

The thought of what would have happened to this little life had we not heard about her made me shudder. The Karen are so bound by their fears that it causes them to do the unthinkable— even burying an infant alive. Their fear drives them to do almost anything to avoid trouble from the spirit world, but no matter how hard they try, they never attain the peace they want. The spirits are never satisfied, always demanding more sacrifices or appeasement.

We could not wait to tell them about Jesus Christ, the ultimate sacrifice, who made eternal peace with God for us. One day we would know enough of the language to share with them about God, the Creator of the universe, who desires that every person's life be filled with joy and peace, wrapped in His arms of love.

Chapter 10

Signs of Life

When Not Tu was first exposed to Christianity, he was single and didn't think about it or realize it could benefit him. After he was married and the responsibility of his wife began to weigh on him, he began to think about the things he had heard. Scott influenced Not Tu's life as he could see how Scott depended on God and was not bound by fear of the spirits. He also saw a joy in Scott that was missing from his own life.

Not Tu and his wife, Mung Me, had been married two years. Like most Pwo Karen couples, they wanted to have children right away, but had experienced two miscarriages during the first year and a half they were together. To appease the spirits, they had performed many ceremonies, their wrists layered with white string revealing their efforts. Wondering if the miscarriages were punishment for breaking some taboo, the young couple had even tried to redo the pig sacrifice that had been done at their wedding in case some small detail had been missed or was not done quite right.

New Christians

When Mung Me became pregnant a third time she and Not Tu were very careful not to break any taboos. They lived in fear that once again something would go wrong and did not want to be bound to more ceremonies. However, as the baby grew and Mung Me's belly protruded, they became more hopeful that this pregnancy would go full-term. Nevertheless, new fears began to lurk as the couple looked forward to the birth of their baby. They had seen many infants die in the village for no apparent reason and worried they would lose this child to illness or some mysterious death.

Not Tu's brothers, who called themselves Christians, had found relief from the sicknesses that had plagued them. They had no understanding of the gospel and salvation by faith, and only followed the form of Christianity by meeting on Sundays to sing and pray. Gle La and his wife had two healthy young boys by this time, and even though Jo Tu was still in jail, Chuu Gee and her children were well again. These two families were now free to go to the hospital in Maesariang when they were sick without first consulting the spirits.

A few weeks before their baby was born, Not Tu and Mung Me decided to join his brothers and become worshipers of God, so they began meeting with them on Sundays. Not Tu already knew the songs and how to pray. He was also the only one who knew how to read, so he would read something from the Pwo Karen New Testament every Sunday.

Another New Life

Early one afternoon, Not Tu came looking for me and asked if I could go to his house to look at his wife. She was having contractions and he didn't know if the baby would deliver normally or if she needed to go to the hospital.

I told Not Tu that I could go, and then turned to Scott and asked him if he could keep the boys while I went to see how Not Tu's wife was progressing. Scott assured me that all would be well with him and the boys, and then added, "I'll pray for you."

I thanked Scott and then grabbed my latex gloves, a few medicines, a clean wash rag and a small blanket and shoved it into my cloth bag. After a short walk through the village with Not Tu, we climbed the ladder and went inside. His wife was in the usual birthing position and looked very uncomfortable. I smiled at her and found a suitable spot beside her on the floor. I asked what questions I knew, adding the new vocabulary I had learned since my last such house call. I was able to determine that the baby's head was indeed down and she was making progress. As I sat beside her, I gently laid my hand on her belly keeping an eye on my watch to time the contractions.

When I mentioned to Not Tu that squeezing her belly would not make the baby come any faster, he believed me and let go of his tight grip around his wife's middle—I felt relieved for her. Every minute or so she would fidget and shift her hands to get a new grip. She was becoming weary of holding onto the rope above her head. As she shifted her weight from one side to the other and back again, often leaning forward to relieve the pressure on her toes it was obvious that she was wearing out. After thirty minutes of this her feet began cramping from being folded under her so I suggested she lay down for a while.

With a concerned look on her face she asked if the baby would still come out if she was lying down. I assured here that the baby would come out fine as I had delivered all of my babies lying down.

Exhausted, she agreed to try; I was glad to see they were willing to listen. After a little while, her contractions became much more intense, and I knew the baby would soon arrive. With help she got to her knees, grabbed the rope above her head and held on tight. The kettle of hot water I had asked for when I first arrived was no longer hot, so I asked Not Tu to stoke the fire again.

While Not Tu worked on the fire, Mung Me began to push. The baby was coming, so I slipped on my gloves and soon was holding a squealing, squirming baby girl, showing her to Not Tu and Mung Me. Both looked pleased and glad to meet their precious little daughter. This was quite a change from the first baby I had delivered where I saw no joy or interest in the newborn.

Finding nowhere clean to put the baby down, I changed my position on the floor so my lap was flat and laid her there on my skirt. Her scream quieted to a cry when she felt the warmth of my body through the skirt. Now it was time to cut the cord. After learning the traditions and customs of the Pwo Karen people, I knew it was a man's job.

I looked at Not Tu and said, "You can cut the cord now."

He looked at me surprised and said, "I've never done that before. I don't know what to do."

I raised my eyebrows in disbelief and said, "I've never done it before either."

Breaking Old Taboos

I wonder what Mung Me was thinking. She may have been exhausted, but it still must have unnerved her a bit to hear us telling each other we didn't know what we were doing! My lack of experience, however, didn't seem to deter Not Tu in any way. He quickly grabbed a hatchet from the floor near the fire box, and a stone nearby. Handing them both to me, he told me that I should cut it. Laying the tools down, I took a moment to think about what I was doing and silently prayed for wisdom:

> *"Lord I don't know what I'm doing here, or even why I'm in this position right now, but I need wisdom. I don't know what to do. Lord, please help me. Help me to remember what I need to do. Thank You, Lord."*

Because Not Tu and his wife were calling themselves Christians, they no longer felt obligated to adhere to the traditional beliefs and taboos of the culture. He didn't feel pressure to be the one to cut the cord because he was free of the bondage of the village spirits. This was faith! He didn't even understand the gospel yet, but he was stepping out in faith that God would take care of them, and not allow the ramifications of breaking taboos cause them hardship.

God seemed to give me clarity of mind and the confidence to proceed, so I had Not Tu bring me two strings from his wife's weaving supplies. I was unsure how far up the cord I needed to tie the strings, so I decided to tie the first just an inch or so from the baby and the other just two inches from that. As I tied, I knew the knots needed to be tight enough to cut off the blood supply, but not so tight they cut into the cord. After making double knots in each piece, the string was still plenty long, so I wrapped it around one more time and tied it again. It looked okay to me, so using the smooth stone I had been given earlier, I held it under the cord, picked up the hatchet and began sawing. The cord kept rolling off the stone as I cut, and the hatchet was dull. Finally, it was done. I saw no bleeding in the end of the cord, so I hoped it meant that the string was tight enough.

Not Tu poured the hot water into a basin and mixed it with cold water to make it warm. Dipping the wash cloth into it I cleaned the baby. Finally, I wrapped her in the small blanket I had brought and handed her off to her daddy. He quickly took her from me, holding her awkwardly like the typical new dad. I spent the next few minutes with Mung Me. She delivered the placenta without any problems and since I had gloves on, I offered to dispose of it as I had seen done at the last house. Not Tu put the baby down and went down out of the house and cut a short tube of bamboo. I put the placenta into the tube and he covered the top of it with a small rag. Reaching into the rafters of the house, he pulled down a bundle of thin bamboo strips that were stored there. Using one of the strips he fastened it around the top of the tube to keep the cloth in place.

I helped clean Mung Me while Not Tu brought her a clean skirt to put on. As she pulled it down under herself, Not Tu and I took the soiled one out. With a fresh skirt on, we helped her lean against a leg of the drying rack that straddled the fire box. Not Tu then filled a brown, flat whisky bottle with hot water and plugged up the end. She used this on her tummy as a heating pad just as the first woman had done with the hot stone. I checked the baby again and made sure the cord was not bleeding and then went home.

When I arrived, I shared with Scott how God had put in my mind what to do and how I had to cut the cord with a rock and hatchet. I knew I did not want to have to cut an umbilical cord with a dirty instrument ever again, so I added to my supply list: medical scissors, clamps and some sterile umbilical ties.

Breaking with Tradition

Two days later Not Tu came to our house asking for medicine for their baby. My heart sank, *Oh no!* I thought. There are so many things that threaten a baby's life at that age, and I hoped that it was not serious.

"What's wrong?" Scott asked.

"Our mosquito net caught fire this morning and it melted and dripped on her face." Not Tu answered. He showed us a burn on his hand from where he had grabbed the net and snuffed out the flame.

Scott and I felt sorry for them. They had trusted God, and now bad things were happening. We didn't know what they were thinking and wondered if this would drive them back to spirit worship. Leaving the boys with Chuu Gee, we went over to their house taking medicine with us. Right beside the corner of the baby's mouth was a serious burn. It was about an inch and a half long and half an inch wide, running vertically beside her mouth. We cleaned it and put burn cream on it trying not to get any in her mouth. We left them with more supplies to clean it and treat it twice daily, and showed them what to do.

"People tell us that we need to do a sacrifice to appease the spirits," Not Tu began, "but we told them that we worship God now, and that we don't need to sacrifice any more. We know that the medicine you bring can heal her burn without doing any of the spirit sacrifices. God can take care of us." Scott and I were very relieved to hear his faith. We were unsure what he was putting his faith in because he knew so little about God.

"God *will* take care of you, and you don't need to do spirit ceremonies. It's not the spirits that make you sick" Scott assured them.

As we walked home, we discussed our burden to share the gospel with them. Our language ability was still far from sufficient to share spiritual truths and be clearly understood. We certainly did not want to confuse them with a muddled Gospel message or a misconstrued idea of the truth. It was clear that God was doing a work in their hearts before we were even ready to begin the work that He had brought us here to do.

When we shared all of this with our co-workers, we were overjoyed by the fact that God was setting the stage right before our eyes. And we, being nothing in ourselves, would be used as a small part of His plan to bring a group of people unto Himself that would ultimately glorify Him.

Chapter 11

Rags to Riches

One day, a truck belonging to a Thai merchant who had been selling fish in the area pulled up in front of our house. I watched as a woman was helped out of the back by her husband and brother. They were in search of medical help for the woman, and like so many others, had come to us asking for assistance. The woman was quite weak, so instead of having her climb the stairs into the house, I suggested she rest in the shade under the porch.

I asked the husband what was wrong with his wife and where she hurt. He said that she'd had dysentery for several days, but had been sick with fever for the past ten days. Then he asked if we could take her to the hospital. I assured him that Scott would as soon as he returned home.

The woman looked dehydrated; her lips were dry and her eyes sunken. I quickly went into the house and prepared a re-hydration drink for her and then helped her take a few sips. She was visibly weaker than just a few minutes earlier; her breathing seemed labored and I noticed a rattling noise in her chest as she breathed.

Seeking Help

Earlier in the day, the woman's brother had come to our house seeking help for her. Scott had just returned from a four-hour round trip to the hospital. Because of this, and the fact that the seriousness of her condition was unknown to us, Scott asked her brother to go see if the headman from our village could give him a ride. A few hours later we were told that he never asked the headman but walked home instead. Scott regretted sending the man away and immediately mounted his motorbike and rode the six or seven miles to the village of Paa Ang. He wanted to see if the woman truly needed to go to the hospital, or if she just needed medication that we had on hand.

The roads are windy and rough so it was much faster for Scott to go by motorbike on the lower road than by truck. Meanwhile, the Thai merchant had agreed to bring the woman, her husband and brother to our house by way of the upper road, which was more suitable for trucks. When Scott arrived at their village and discovered that she was no longer there, he quickly turned around and headed home.

As soon as Scott arrived we discussed the woman's condition. We both knew that she needed to be in the hospital and would likely need to stay for several days. As the couple and her brother were getting settled in the back of the truck, one of our neighbors asked them where their baby was. "At home," the husband replied. That surprised me, so I inquired further.

"You have a baby at home? How old is it?"

"Just two months," he said.

Because of his wife's condition I knew that their trip to the hospital would take them away from the baby for several days. "Who will care for the baby while you are away," I asked?

"Her grandma," he said. I knew this was not good because the Karen have no access to formula or any type of baby food. The baby would be given water and rice chewed up by the grandmother. This kind of diet would not be nourishing and I worried that the baby's health would decline by the time the parents returned home.

Preparing for Baby

I told the man that if they had brought the baby along, the nurses at the hospital would have fed it until the mother was better, or I could have cared for it until they returned. He suggested that when Scott returned from the hospital he could get the baby so we could care for it until they came home.

I talked to Scott and asked him to pick up some formula and bottles so we could care for the baby until the parents returned. He agreed and then said he would be home around nine o'clock that night.

We said our goodbyes and then I stepped away so he could be on his way. I watched as they went down the hill from the house, around the corner and out of the village, and then whispered, *Lord, please help them make it to the hospital.* I knew Scott was tired as he had already made this trip once today. I hated to see him go again, but knew that this woman's life depended on it.

I fixed supper for the boys, wondering the whole time what it was going to be like having a baby in the house again. Seth was now three, Joel and Daniel were five and six, so it had been a while since I had to get up in the night to feed a little one. Even so, it would be fun to take care of a baby for a few days. The boys were excited, too. We ate supper and cleaned up, and then I lit the fire to heat water for our showers.

Another Life Taken

Scott called me on the radio just as I was getting the kids ready for bed. He said that he was in Meahot getting formula. My heart sank when he told me that the woman had died on the way to the hospital. Then Scott told me that the villagers in Taa Fai wouldn't let them carry her body back through their village so the husband and brother were burying her while Scott went into town for formula.

Oh, my. I thought to myself, holding back the tears. *Those poor men, having to bury her right there, in a village so far from home!* The woman's husband and brother were the only ones at her funeral. Her mother and father didn't even know that she was gone, and she was already in the burial grounds. The two men would be returning without her.

I gathered the boys around me and told them what had happened. I didn't know what this would mean for the baby, and didn't even know if it was a boy or girl. Karen language pronouns do not have a gender like our English "him" or "her." In my earlier conversations with the father there was no indication of "boy" or "girl."

Scott and the two Karen men arrived back at our home around nine thirty. They all came in the house looking physically and emotionally exhausted, the two men sitting on the floor near the door. "Do you still want us to care for your baby tonight?" Scott asked the husband.

"Yes. I can't take care of the baby," he responded.

"We could even take care of it for two weeks while you and your family decide what to do" Scott offered. "If you were to decide that you want us to raise the child, we are willing to do that, but we will adopt it as our own and not give it back." Scott clarified. The father said that he wanted Scott to pick up the baby that night so we could care for it until they made a decision.

Little Baby Girl

I couldn't stand it any more and had to ask, "Is it a boy or a girl?"

"A girl" he said.

My heart leapt a bit. I knew the boys would be happy too.

Daniel asked if he could go along with daddy, and his wish was granted. Scott also asked Dite Moi to accompany him. Scott handed me the bottles and formula he had gotten and said we had better get things ready and to have Joel help me.

They all went out the door into the darkness with only Scott's flashlight to light the way. Soon I heard the truck start and then climb the steep hill beside our house, driving into the night.

Seth was asleep by this time, so Joel and I started getting things ready. We boiled the bottles and got out the cloth diapers, pins and plastic pants from storage. Having no baby clothes, we started looking through Seth's clothes for something small and found a few T-shirts to use. It was all we had, so it would have to do. Our final job was to get out the port-a-crib, sheets and blankets. Then Joel and I sat down to wait for them to return.

It was now almost midnight and I could tell that Joel was sleepy though not ready to go to bed. He wanted to see this new little baby girl we were bringing into our home. I had to explain to him that we were not keeping her, just taking care of her for two weeks. We knew that the family may ask us to take her as our own, but we didn't want the boys to get their hopes up. For now, we told them she was just with us for two weeks.

It seemed like a long time before we heard the truck coming back down the hill. Scott stopped right next to our porch and Dite Moi got out and handed a bundle to me.

Baby's Home

She was sound asleep and wrapped in a dirty grey blanket. Anxious to see her little face, I pulled back some of the fabric so I could get a look and then knelt down to show Joel. He grinned, held his finger to his lips and said, "Shhhh, she's asleep." It was evident that he was thrilled to have her here. Daniel wanted to see as well. It had been so dark on their trip that he hadn't gotten to see her.

Scott parked the truck and came up the stairs into the house. We all stood around getting a good look at her before deciding what to do. She was sleeping so soundly we decided not to unwrap her but just let her sleep. I suggested that we lay her in a little plastic bathtub, blanket and all. She fit into it perfectly, so we set the tub on the couch on the other side of our bedroom wall. Since our walls were not much thicker than paper, we would be able to easily hear her when she awakened. Then we gathered around her while Scott prayed:

> Lord, thank-You for safe travel today. I pray that You would comfort this little one's family tonight and that they would one day know You as their Savior. I pray that Your will would be done concerning this baby. Give us all a good night's sleep. Amen.

We all went to bed, but I had not been asleep long when the baby began to cry. I got up and fixed a bottle as quickly as I could, but she was crying pretty hard by the time I had the bottle ready. I picked her up and sat down in the rocking chair. The bottom of the blanket was wet, but I decided to try feeding her first. I was not sure that she would take a bottle since that would be a new experience for her. I made four ounces thinking that she may drink half of it, but she must have been very hungry. She drank the whole thing, hardly stopping to take a breath. She seemed very happy with a full tummy, so I took the opportunity to open up the large blanket and put a diaper on her and wrapped her in a clean baby blanket. She desperately needed a bath, but that would have to wait until morning. She was getting sleepy again, so I put her down in the crib in our room and went back to sleep.

In the morning, many of our neighbors came to see her and the boys all wanted to hold her. The creases in her neck and wrists were caked with dirt and she smelled of wood smoke, however with the boys' help I got her all washed up and smelling clean. Then I dressed her in one of Seth's shirts, which came down to her ankles. She was adorable!

Our family adjusted to having a baby in the house again and we reminded ourselves not to get too attached since this may be temporary. Therefore, we decided not to name her before we knew whether she would be staying or not.

Trusting God

Just four months prior we had cared for a newborn whose mother had died in childbirth. After only two days her father returned for her. We had sent bottles and formula with him and instructed him on how to use and clean them. Nevertheless, word came from the distant village that the baby had died only two weeks later. We were grieved at the easily preventable loss of life and didn't want that to ever happen again, but that was out of our control. We prayed and trusted God to work in the hearts of the family and to make a good decision for the baby.

Nearly a week went by. Then one morning one of our neighbors came to tell us that Nane Jee was in the village. When we asked who that was, the neighbor said it was the baby's father.

"He has come to take the baby home. The grandmother wants her back." Our hearts sank. *Oh no, not again.* We thought.

We waited and waited for him to come to our house to tell us, but hours went by and he did not show up. Finally, Scott could wait no longer so he set out to find Nane Jee. It wasn't hard. Our friends and neighbors had him surrounded telling him that he would be wrong to take the baby home.

"The baby will die, and the sin will be on you," they told him. "You need to do what is best for the baby, don't be selfish. Grandma can't take care of the baby and you know it. You're her father, you make the decision." With that, he left the village and headed for home and never came to ask for her. Scott didn't have to say anything to him.

When Scott returned home, we were still uncertain that a final decision had been made. One of our neighbors came up to our house later to make sure that we understood correctly that Nane Jee wanted us to keep the baby and raise her as our own. Our language ability was still lacking in some areas, so Scott hadn't fully understood the situation. It was clear now though, that we had become a family of six, providing the adoption would be approved. We knew the adoption process would be long and time consuming, but it didn't dampen our spirits. We trusted God to intervene for us just as He always does.

We were thrilled to have her as our own and began talking about names. The boys even had suggestions, but we finally settled on Bethany Grace. Many months later when we finally had an opportunity to look at a name book, the meaning for Bethany was, "To be brought out of poverty." It gave me goose bumps, because it was by the grace of God that she was brought out of poverty into wealth. Not so much material wealth, but spiritual. She would be taught about God the Creator and His love for her and she would learn that Almighty God sent His Son, Jesus, to earth, and that Jesus died so that she might spend eternity with Him.

Chapter 12

Spiritual Awakening

Around the low flicker of the fire inside a small bamboo hut, children and adults sat on the floor in complete silence listening to an old man. His face was creased with deep wrinkles and his short hair was mostly gray. He sat Indian style near the fire box on a straw mat, his back slightly arched with age. He was a traveler, who walked from village to village staying for several days. People begged him to stay in their homes, feeding him and giving him a place to sleep in exchange for hours of enchanting stories. It was a treat to convince a good story teller to entertain them. Late into the night, the younger children fought to stay awake to hear the end of the story. The listeners hung on his every word as the climax of the story captivated them.

Superstitions and the Story Teller

Quietly, the story teller began…

One day god was out working in his field when Satan, (a woman) came to tempt god. She tried to get god to go home and sleep with her. But god resisted the temptation and told Satan to go away because he already had a wife. Satan was not so quick to give up, and she tried over and over to get god to sleep with her. Finally Satan formed a plan. She collected her whisky from home and brought it to god offering him a drink. The two of them had one after another until god became drunk and Satan took advantage of god. In the next few months that followed, Satan discovered that she was pregnant with god's child.....

He enchanted the group for hours with legends as well as some of his own made-up stories.

Some of the stories told around the fire revealed the horrors of walking through burial grounds and being attacked by the spirits of the dead or by demons. For the Karen people it was a scary place to go even with a large group in broad daylight; it was unthinkable to go near it alone or at night.

Entertaining stories and traditional legends were all passed down from generation to generation in this manner. Stories of a creator being, a Satan figure and a couple from whom all humans originate, heroes and monsters are all part of their folklore. Depending upon the story teller, the stories change over the years as details are added or forgotten.

Legends of God

The old man took a puff of his hand-made wooden pipe and began another story. "There were several brothers. The eldest brother was a Karen and the youngest was a white man. God had a book that he wanted to give to the older Karen brother so that they could have the truth; it was called the good, white book. One day god brought this holy book to give it to the older Karen brother but he was busy cooking snails. He told god that his snails were not soft yet and he couldn't come out and get the book so he asked god to leave it outside on the stump."

Some legends that the people believe say that a pig came along and ate the book. When the pig later passed it, a chicken came along scratching in the pig dung and re-ate the book. Because of this, these people believe that truth is found in the bones of chickens. This is why the spirit-men of the village use chicken bones to divine with the spirits. They believe the bones will reveal the truth. Other legends say the younger white brother ended up with the book and that one day he will return and bring god's holy book back to the Karen people.

It was clear to us that the Karen understanding of God was either warped or completely false. They believed He could be deceived and tricked, and He was portrayed as mortal with a human body, wife and parents. Their misinterpretation of this creator being, termed "god", would need to be corrected as we unfolded the true Word of God for them.

Teaching the Truth

After three years of language and culture study, Scott's language ability became proficient enough to communicate biblical and spiritual truth. God had blessed Scott with a special ability to learn and retain language. In preparation for teaching, he spent the next eight months translating Bible lessons into Karen following the lesson plan laid out by New Tribes Mission. He began with the character of God and the creation of the world, then moved through the Old Testament and ended with the life of Christ; a total of sixty eight lessons.

When most of the lessons were ready, Scott began to visit people in their homes to spark interest in hearing truth from God's Holy Book. As he sat on the porch with one older woman, he began asking her questions. "What will happen to you when you die?" he asked her.

"I will go to the village of the dead, and all my friends will be there," she explained.

"How do you know this is true?"

"My parents told me so."

"How did they know about this? How can you be sure this is the truth," Scott asked?

"I don't know," she said.

"In a few weeks I will begin teaching from the Holy Book that comes from God. What God says is always true, because he knows everything and created everything. If you want to know what the Book says, you can come and listen. Then you will know the truth, about life after death," Scott explained.

Klow Kang

Scott made his way around the village talking to anyone who would listen, asking the same type of questions and telling them that he would soon begin teaching about God the creator and His Holy Book. As he went from house to house he stopped at one particular house and talked to a man named Klow Kang. He was a loud, confident man who was respected among the villagers and very knowledgeable in the traditions and customs of his people. Both Klow Kang and his father listened intently.

"The Holy Book is God's message to man," Scott explained. "Soon I will be starting to teach from the Book. Anyone who wants to listen can come."

Klow Kang and his father were both very interested in learning about the truth and God's message to man. They wanted to know what the Book said about what happens to a man's soul when he dies and the truth about Satan and the demons that they followed.

At the time, we had no idea what God was doing in the hearts of each individual. However, God was answering our prayers working behind the scenes to prepare the hearts of the people to be reached with the gospel. When Scott finally began teaching, Klow Kang's interest in the Bible and in learning the truth drove him to attend every session. These meetings were held in one of the Thai school classrooms because it was a neutral location. That way, no one would feel they were being pegged as a Christian if they attended. We felt that this would reach more people than just meeting with the group who were already claiming to be Christians or just teaching on Sunday mornings.

On the first night of teaching we were amazed because about ninety people showed up to listen. Though it was only about ten percent of the village population, it was more than we expected.

Scott taught two or three nights each week. The fourth lesson was about how God created the angels and how the head angel, Lucifer, sinned and turned away from God. Scott told them how Lucifer became known as Satan and the angels who followed him became the demons.

As Klow Kang sat listening, he absorbed this new knowledge about the Creator God's authority and power over the spirit beings that had held him in bondage by fear since he was a child. "Don't go here, don't go there," his parents had taught him. "The spirits will eat you."

When Scott finished teaching that night, Klow Kang came up to him and said, "Why have we been so afraid of the spirits? We have been foolish. I would go to the burial grounds now and spend the night by myself," he said with confidence! "Since God is more powerful, He can protect me in any situation."

Klow Kang's faith amazed us! He had only heard four lessons and knew only a few of God's innumerable attributes, yet he believed them to the point of tossing aside the old ingrained belief system that formed his entire world view. The truth was setting him free from the reign and control of evil spirits in his life and now he could trust God to protect him even in the burial grounds.

Every new lesson built on the next and Klow Kang drank them in like a parched man on a hot dusty road. He gulped it down and yearned for more as if he had been searching for the truth for a long time and finally found it.

Each evening Scott handed out a copy of the lesson in Karen to those who could read. Klow Kang took one each time even though he could not read. He was so zealous about this new-found truth, that with the help of one of his kids, he taught himself to read so he could review the lesson then tell his wife, children, parents and neighbors about it.

God's Character Revealed

He shared with them what he had learned about the character of God, about creation, Satan's deception of Eve, mankind's sin and the separation from God that man experienced because of that sin. Being born from a sinful man, the whole human race was born with a sinful nature and could only make atonement for that sin by the sacrifice of a perfect lamb. The Old Testament characters were required to make this sacrifice to God often in obedience which revealed their dependence upon God and their belief in the coming Deliverer.

As Scott revealed more and more of the Bible stories in chronological order, he kept reminding the group of the promise God had made to Adam and Eve of the Deliverer that would come to make atonement for their sins. The Deliverer would be sent by God and would make the ultimate sacrifice to offer all mankind an everlasting relationship with God and eternity in heaven.

The loving character of God was revealed through creation, in which God created a perfect environment for man, gave him a woman as a help mate, and walked with Adam and Eve in the garden. Even after man's sin, God's love for the human race was evident in the promise of a Deliverer.

God's obvious grace was woven through every story as God dealt with an undeserving mankind. He chose the nation Israel as His people by which the rest of the world would come to know Him. By grace, Noah and his family escaped the flood, and Sarah bore a child in her old age. God's power was displayed in creation, the plagues in Egypt, parting the Red Sea, and 40 years of providing for the nation of Israel in the wilderness to name a few.

The fact that God knows all things was a new concept to Klow Kang and the group that listened to the Bible stories. The spirits they worshiped could be deceived, but they learned that God knew the thoughts and intentions of man whether it be a silent prayer or an evil plot. Nothing could be hidden from God and He is perfect and holy.

Klow Kang also learned through the stories of the people in Noah's day, the tower of Babel, the Egyptians, Sodom and Gomorrah, and that there was punishment for unbelief. In each of these stories the characters who believed God and His plan for deliverance were spared judgment. By faith, Abel offered a pleasing sacrifice to God, by faith Noah entered through the single door of the ark and was saved from the destruction of the world by water. Lot was spared from the fiery destruction of Sodom and Gomorrah because he was righteous through his faith in God. By faith, the Israelites, when they were slaves in Egypt, killed an unblemished lamb and spread its blood on their door posts so the angel of death would pass them over, sparing their firstborn from death. And by faith Moses led the Israelites to freedom from being enslaved to a cruel Egyptian Pharaoh.

Nurturing Faith

Scott spent three months telling the stories that laid the foundation of God's character and how He dealt with mankind. He always kept before the people God's promise of a Deliverer who would come to make a sacrifice to cover everyone's sin for all eternity.

As the group met night after night, week after week, the number of people attending dwindled to ten or twelve. Among the few that remained was Klow Kang with his energetic enthusiasm, Not Tu, who for the first time was beginning to understand what the "church thing" and Christianity was all about, Klow Kang's father and Chuu Gee. Each attended faithfully and learned about God's character and His promises written in the Bible.

Not Kwat, another young man who came to the teaching, had been trained and hired as a literacy teacher like Not Tu and was one of the few adults who could read and write. His father was the spirit-headman of Maepae and was highly respected in the village for his spiritual wisdom. Many people went to him to find answers for their spiritual questions. The welfare of the village rested upon his shoulders as it was up to him to ensure that all the spirit ceremonies were done correctly and every village problem solved through divination and sacrifices according to his direction.

Not Kwat grew up in this atmosphere and was well versed in the traditions and customs of his people. He was unsatisfied, however, and searching for real truth. Before Scott began teaching, Not Kwat often went and talked with Harry who told him about God, and shared that God was all knowing, all powerful and eternal. Not Kwat was surprised to learn that God was more powerful than the spirits he had watched his father worship and appease.

Not Kwat was so interested in knowing about the Bible and the truths it contained that he disregarded his father's wishes and sat under the teaching of the Bible, learning all that he could. Every time Scott taught, he would sneak out or tell his parents he was going to visit someone, but then went straight to the meeting area to hear God's message to man from the Bible.

As Not Kwat listened to the story of Adam and Eve he learned that the penalty for sin is death. During the story of Cain and Abel, Not Kwat learned about God's requirement for animal sacrifice. He learned that the only acceptable sacrifice was a perfect lamb and he began to worry about where he could find a lamb to offer. Sacrifices were not foreign to the Karen culture. He had witnessed the sacrifices of pigs and chickens often, and his father was in charge of the sacrifice of the white water buffalo which took place every three years. Not Kwat was anxious to find the right type of sacrifice to appease God and to bridge the gap between himself and the righteous and holy God he was beginning to know. He had never seen a lamb and realized he would not be able to make an acceptable sacrifice, so he held onto the hope that the Deliverer whom God promised would make a way for him to be accepted.

The Promised Deliverer

From the time Adam and Eve disobeyed and sin separated them from God, a Deliverer had been promised who would restore the people to relationship with their creator. As long as they depended upon the coming Deliverer and displayed that dependence with periodic animal sacrifices, they enjoyed fellowship with God and the assurance of eternity with Him. As Scott told the stories, he kept reminding them of the Deliverer God had promised.

Only a handful of people remained committed to attending the teaching, yet these individuals were attentive and understood every lesson as it was taught. All were curious to see who the Deliverer was and what would be done to liberate them from the bonds of sin and death.

After eight or nine weeks of laying the foundation about God and His dealings with mankind through Old Testament stories, Scott told them the story of Jesus, God's only son who was born of a virgin. This was the Messiah, the Deliverer, the fulfillment of the promise. It was what they had all been waiting for.

As Scott continued through the stories about Jesus, the listeners were not surprised that Jesus was loving, could do miracles, or that he knew the thoughts of men. They had been taught from the very first chapter in the Bible that the Father and the Son were one therefore all the attributes of God also applied to His Son. Even though Jesus had human form, He was holy, all knowing, all powerful, kind, loving, gentle and absolutely perfect. They could not, however, understand how men could have treated Him so poorly; trying to trick Him, scheming to turn others against Him and having no place to lay his head.

Just two lessons before Scott was to present the gospel, Not Kwat came to our house. He said that he had to leave and find work in Chiangmai the next morning and wouldn't get to hear the rest of the Bible lessons. Then he asked if Scott would teach them to him before he left.

Scott agreed and the two of them sat down at the kitchen table. Scott began with the story of the last supper and how Jesus foretold Judas' betrayal and Peter's denial. Scott told about Gethsemane and Jesus' prayer to the Father, then the arrest of Jesus in the garden and his trial. Not Kwat sat listening with a concerned look on his face. I could imagine what he was thinking. *But this is the Messiah. This is the Son of God who was sent to deliver us. They can't hurt Him. God will protect His Son. Satan is causing all of this trouble. God will win this battle because He is more powerful than Satan.*

Not Kwat listened in dismay at the story of the crowd yelling, "Crucify Him! Crucify Him!" Then he listened as Scott told of the brutal death and burial of Jesus Christ. Jesus allowed the men to kill him. He had power over them, but He did not stop them. It seemed to Not Kwat like the end of the story.

Scott continued:

> *On Sunday morning the women went out to the tomb with spices to put on the body. When they arrived there, they found the large stone rolled away and the tomb open. When they went inside, His body was not there. Then two angels appeared and asked them, 'Why do you look for the living among the dead? He is not here; He has risen!'*
>
> *You see, Jesus could not be conquered by death. If He had stayed in the tomb, He would be no different than any man who died, and He would not be the Savior. Jesus Himself became the perfect sacrifice that saved all mankind, and restored our broken relationship with God. Jesus was the lamb, the one who died once for all, so that all of us might live in heaven with God. The penalty for sin is death, and He became sin; and died that we could be saved.*
>
> *You see, Satan thought he had won and destroyed the Deliverer, but he actually assisted God in His plan and through Jesus' death all men can be saved. The sacrifice of a lamb is no longer required, only faith in Jesus Christ's death as our substitute. He was raised to life, having victory over death and the grave.*

Scott told him how the disciples saw Jesus and spent time with Him after His resurrection and then witnessed his ascension into heaven. Jesus now sits at the right hand of God the Father in heaven.

God's Children

When Scott was finished, Not Kwat sat for a moment nodding his head in deep thought. "So Jesus Christ was the sacrifice and there are no more to make? It's all finished?"

"Yes, that's right. Anyone who believes in this sacrifice as atonement for their sin will be accepted as God's child and their soul will spend eternity with Him in heaven."

A smile came over Not Kwat's face and he said, "Then I am God's child and my soul will live in heaven with Him forever."

As I listened to all of this, I couldn't help but feel like shouting across the mountains to let everyone know that there was a soul saved in Maepae! I could hardly contain my joy.

After Not Kwat left, Scott and I looked at each other, both grinning from ear to ear. We hugged each other and thanked God for the miracle. This is what we had hoped and prayed so many years for.

Two nights later Scott told the same story to the group that he had been teaching in the evenings. Not Tu, Chuu Gee, Klow Kang and his father all came to know Jesus Christ as their Savior that night, by faith. Five had been added to the family of God, and our hearts were bursting with joy and excitement.

God had prepared each of their hearts in different ways. He had used different circumstances and desires to cultivate hearts ready to hear His Word. We were excited when ninety people came to listen to the first lesson, and tempted to become discouraged when the numbers decreased night after night until there were only a few. But we felt these five were hand-picked by God. Three of the men could read and write, one of whom was the son of the spirit headman.

Klow Kang was bold and well liked. Not Tu and Chee Gee were our first Karen friends.

From my favorite spot on our porch I looked up and noticed that the plant growing from the top of the dead tree had grown a lot in the four years since we had moved there. The parasitic tentacles at the base of the plant had begun to make their way down the trunk of the dead tree latched on by spidery veins extending from each tentacle. The new life of this plant was beginning to cover the old dead tree trunk. The leaves even provided a little shade over our porch. *Maybe this ugly tree had potential after all,* I thought. *It could provide some shade for the porch.*

New life had also begun in the lives of five Karen people; the life of Christ. A new life in Christ would take the place of the old. As the truth progressively replaced the old way of thinking with the new in the lives of these new believers, and as they grew in their relationship with God, they would become more and more conformed to the image of Christ. Displaying the life of Christ for all to see and bringing more people into the Kingdom.

Chapter 13

Passing the Baton

Of the families who were meeting on Sunday mornings, only Chuu Gee and Not Tu attended the evening meetings and now understood what this "Christian" thing was all about. They understood that Christ was the ultimate sacrifice made for the restoration of all mankind. The others who gathered on Sunday mornings had not yet heard the gospel and had very little knowledge of the true character of God.

Our next goal was to teach through the same lessons to the Sunday group who hadn't yet heard the gospel. With Not Kwat and Klow Kang now joining these families for worship we had three men who had been taught and who could read.

New Karen Teachers

Scott felt that these three men understood the truth and could communicate it more clearly than he could to the church group on Sunday mornings. Therefore, the decision was made to involve these three men in teaching.

The task was very difficult for the three of them at first. When they stood to teach, you could see them shaking as they read the lesson out loud. Scott and Harry met with the men during the week to help prepare them for each lesson. They reminded the men to emphasize the character of God as revealed in the story and not just relate the events that took place. As the weeks went by, each man became more comfortable with their teaching role and needed less help.

Little by little more people began to attend the service. Some came because they were sick and the spirits had failed to heal them so they decided to give God a try. One such family came because the woman was suffering from chronic asthma and one of her daughter's had epilepsy. They were seeking relief from their physical afflictions so they came to the church looking for answers.

Chuu Gee's house had more room inside than most Karen homes, so church was held there with everyone sitting on the floor listening to the lessons. Babies crawled around from person to person, playing with whatever interested them and crying from time to time. Dogs would come in only to be shooed back outside; roosters crowed...I wondered how anyone could get anything out of the teaching, but most of them seemed to understand.

Sharing the Gospel

Finally the morning that they were to present the gospel had come and our team was excited to see what would happen. The numbers had increased from just a few families to about sixty individuals, each coming for different reasons. Some were seeking physical relief and others were seeking freedom from the bondage of fear.

When we arrived at Chuu Gee's house that Sunday morning, Klow Kang told us that there would be a wedding taking place next door and all the noise would be a huge distraction. The Karen play drums and cymbals all day long during the wedding, and people get drunk and rowdy. As we talked about what to do, Klow Kang said, "God will take care of it."

We began our meeting as usual and everyone listened intently. I must admit that I expected the drums to begin at any moment and interrupt the teaching, but it never happened. I have never witnessed a virtually silent Pwo Karen wedding before or since that day.

Not Tu was teaching that morning. Fully understanding the importance of the message, he wanted to make sure nothing was missed, so he asked Scott to take over about half-way through. Scott stood and held up the picture of the three crosses and told the group what Jesus had done for them. The people were captivated. Relief came across their faces as Jesus conquered death, rose from the grave and ascended into heaven to sit at God's right hand.

> *"God did this to atone for your sinfulness. He did it so you could be His child, and provide a way for your soul to spend eternity in heaven with Him."*

A Church Begins

Scott paused to let this sink in. Then he asked, "Who believes this?" Immediately a resounding "Me!" came in unison from about fifty people.

This was the birth of the church in the village of Maepae! For our team of three families, it had been five years of labor. We had struggled with the language, the culture and the living conditions, but finally there was a body of believers. Their hearts were made ready by God, just as He forms the life of a child in the womb. He had orchestrated things and circumstances to create a desire and need in the lives of this group. Our team was only a tool in the hand of God to share His Word with a people that were ready to hear.

The asthmatic woman later gave testimony that she no longer wished for physical healing, but looked forward to the day when she was free from her stricken body in heaven. She talked of the hope that she had and of her freedom from fear. A few years later her daughter with epilepsy was the first from the church to be ushered into the presence of her redeemer.

Contagious Faith

When she did not return home from fishing one evening, a search party went out looking for her. A big storm halted the search just after nightfall, but when it resumed the following morning her body was found in a pool of knee deep water. She probably had an epileptic seizure when she was wading in the water, or near the edge. The funeral was unlike any of the traditional ones of the past. The believers buried her in the burial grounds without all of the spiritual rituals and ceremonies. They knew that only her body remained on the earth and that her spirit would not be walking around at night to haunt them.

Traumatic events still occurred in the village, but the believers looked at everything differently. Their trust was in the all-powerful God they were beginning to know. Some time later, Not Tu was involved in a terrible truck accident and sustained a skull fracture that almost took his life. Yet through it all, he and his wife trusted God. He was bombarded by friends and family who told him that the spirits were punishing him for believing in God. Villagers tried hard to get him and his wife to perform spirit ceremonies for quicker healing, but Not Tu and Mung Me held firm. They stood solidly upon their faith in God while unbelievers all around were amazed to see healing take place without multiple ceremonies and sacrifices. This had never been done before, and everyone was watching.

God continued to prepare hearts in the village of Maepae as interest grew and more people attended the church service. Now, the men who were teaching had two different groups to care for;

those who understood the gospel and the newcomers who had not yet heard it. So they split the group in two and taught what was appropriate for their current spiritual state.

Word spread and soon another village showed interest. Not Tu and Klow Kang traveled there several times a week to teach. Then after several months they were able to share the gospel and many were saved. A few years later, people from another village asked to be taught and most of them have also come to a saving knowledge of Jesus Christ. Soon there were scattered believers in five other villages.

God continues to prepare hearts and increase His church. The believers in Maepae are maturing and bringing glory to God through their lives of faith.

Chapter 14

God's Grace Displayed

During the spring of 2002, just eleven years after we moved into the village of Maepae, we felt God leading us to begin the process of leaving the church on its own. As hard as this was to consider, Scott used a verse in John's Gospel to remind me that our original goal was to work ourselves out of a job:

> But I tell you the truth it is for your good that I am going away. Unless I go away, the Counselor will not come to you; but if I go, I will send him to you....I have much more to say to you, more than you can now bear. But when he, the Spirit of truth, comes, he will guide you into all truth. (John 16:7 & 12, 13)

A Very Difficult Day

Though it may seem to have been better for Jesus to stay with the disciples and continue to be an example and teach them, He said that it was better that He leave them. Likewise, the time comes when it is better to leave growing believers on their own to learn from the

Word of God and the conviction of the Holy Spirit, for He promises to lead them into truth. Therefore, after evaluation by New Tribes leadership and their international church planting consultants, it was determined that the church was ready to begin the process of standing on its own feet.

The day the decision was made was a very difficult day. It was exciting to think that God had prepared the way before us and we had done what we had come for, but it had also become our lives, and the thought of leaving was painful. Very much like raising children, we had poured so much time and effort into teaching the Karen, they had become a part of us. As much as we raise our children to become independent, it is still hard to see them go.

Arriving at the decision was difficult, though not as difficult as the day that we actually left and moved to town. It had been our goal from "day 1" to plant a church to be self-supporting, self-propagating and self-governing, an indigenous church no longer needing our constant presence.

The Joy of God's Faithfulness

The help and input of these lovely people into our daily lives helped us learn how to live in those remote and sometimes extreme living conditions. God also gave us many opportunities to help them physically, and to play a part in seeing them brought into the family of God. We have laughed together, played jokes on each other, cried together, gotten angry together (even at each other), and have worshiped and praised God together. These precious ones had become some of our closest and dearest friends. We praised God for the work that He had done in their lives in bringing them to this point, but at the same time, we had grown to love life with our brothers and sisters in Maepae.

Through the years of separation following our leaving, God has continued to allow us to make periodic trips back to visit the church. We have witnessed the joys of seeing the believers mature and become established in their faith. Seeing them function as the body of Christ in their local context far outweighs the sorrow of no longer being with them. The words of John ring very true in our hearts as well: *"I have no greater joy than to hear that my children walk in truth"* (3 John 1:4).

At the time of this writing, the church in Maepae has four key leaders and one younger man in training. These men teach the children, teens, and adults in the Maepae church, work on lesson revisions, Old Testament Bible translation, and have been carrying out the teaching in other villages. Currently (2009) they oversee the teaching in six villages, all of which are at various stages in the church planting process (four of the villages have people meeting as larger groups). This modern day Pwo Karen tribal church has its roots and foundation in the early church in Acts, and is a continuation of the fulfillment of Christ's promise that He will build His church.

During the seven years that we have not lived with them, it's been exciting for us to see and hear about the amazing faithfulness of God as He continues to show Himself strong on their behalf. Just as God led, worked and intervened to establish the early church in the book of Acts, we have seen Him doing that same work in the lives of the Pwo Karen. The believers continue to receive the sound teaching of God's Word, while at the same time God continues to draw more and more unbelievers unto Himself from many of the villages in the area.

God Protects and Shields

These faithful saints have even seen God's protective intervention in the face of strong opposition. One example of this occurred in the village of Pay Zur. The teaching first began in this village around

1998 or 1999 with one family who requested the men from Maepae to come and teach them. The men agreed and began to teach in the village weekly. Soon their neighbors became interested and in a very short period of time there were 8 or 10 households gathering to be taught. Their decision to become Christians meant that these people had left their animistic practices.

The spirit headman of Pay Zur soon realized the financial burden that this would add to the rest of the village. Their animistic belief system requires at times the sacrifice of a large albino water buffalo. The cost of this expensive sacrifice is divided up evenly among the households in the village. Now that 8 or 10 households had left animism to become Christians, the portion each family had to contribute to buy the sacred white water buffalo would increase.

The spirit headman began to talk with the older men in the village, and soon a large number became emboldened enough to oppose the Christian teaching and try to prevent these families from leaving spirit worship. At first the opposition was in the form of snide remarks that were made to the "Christians."

The opposition then escalated to physical acts meant to discourage the teachers from coming to the village. Often while meeting in someone's home, the villagers would throw rocks and sticks onto the tin roof to disturb the teaching. At other times when the teachers finished a meeting they would discover that the air had been let out of their motorcycle tires. The physical opposition escalated even further when the teachers would have things hurled at them while riding into the village to teach.

When snide remarks and physical opposition didn't stop the teaching, the entire village came together and gave the 10 households an ultimatum: *"Either you stop meeting as Christians and come back to following the spirits, or move out of our village and off all the land that belongs to our village."*

This demand was more than the little group in Pay Zur could bear so the teaching was stopped and they no longer met together in their village. Nevertheless, many in this group still came to Maepae on Sunday mornings to attend worship service there.

This continued for a few years until the spirit headman unexpectedly died. The group that claimed to be Christians soon began to meet again. This went on for a few months until a new spirit headman was designated. Unfortunately, he, too, turned the village against the group forcing the teaching and meetings to stop once again. Within two years this spirit headman, who was younger than the first, also unexpectedly died. Normally, the position of spirit headman is somewhat prestigious, but now none of the men in the village were willing to accept the role. They were afraid to take the position so the village went for over a year without anyone willing to do it.

Meeting Once Again

In January of 2009, the church leaders from Maepae went to visit these folks in Pay Zur and to ask if they were ready to begin meeting together again. The people were ready and the men began to travel there twice a week to meet with them. Once again they began teaching through the Scriptures from creation to Christ. The men were surprised to discover that 24 households were now coming to the teaching.

Towards the end of February 2009, Not Tu (one of the Maepae church leaders) called to tell us about everything God had been doing among them. Of the 100 plus houses in the village of Pay Zur, 39 have rejected spirit worship and desire to be taught the Word of God. He said the meetings are packed, and they are convinced that even though the village now has a new spirit headman, he will be unable to force the group to stop meeting again. These precious people are now praising God for His wonderful display of grace and power on the behalf of His children.

This year as I prepare for the Christmas season here in my comfortable home in America with Christmas decorations, gifts to buy and baking to do, my mind often wanders to this little village of Pay Zur half way around the world. Just less than a week before Christmas more than one hundred people gathered to hear the story of Christ's substitutionary death on the cross. With the house full to the brim, tarps were spread on the ground to create extra seating for all who wanted to hear the final message; the climax of the story; the reason Christ came to earth. One hundred people sat intently listening as it was revealed that the deliverer they had waited for, now stood condemned before Pilate and finally was taken to be beaten and crucified, not for any sin that he possessed, but for the sin of mankind. In the coming weeks Not Tu will meet with people individually and it will become clear who has understood the message, but so far it is clear that there are at least thirty new believers. New life in Christ has to be the best Christmas gift ever! Christmas day has come and gone in the village of Pay Zur without a single decoration, wrapped Christmas gift or Christmas candy yet their understanding of the Christmas story is pure and unclouded, and the gift they received will never be stolen, wear out or be used up.

Today, as our family looks back on the little window of 19 years that we have been involved with the Northern Pwo Karen, we realize that they have been on God's heart from before the foundations of the earth were laid. God has numbered the hairs of every one of their heads and He loves them with a love that surpasses all under-standing. You can almost sense His joy and pleasure in the way that He continues to show Himself strong as He faithfully works to continue to build and establish the Pwo Karen church. And it's no wonder, for they are His children, and He is truly their God and heavenly Father!

Lessons from a Dead Tree

On a recent trip back to Thailand, we stayed in our old house. I noticed that the plant on the dead tree near our porch had grown a lot since we moved out. The old dead trunk was almost entirely encased in the thick vines of the parasitic plant.

In the same way, Jesus has conquered sin and death and replaced the old with the new. These Pwo Karen believers have been placed into Jesus Christ and the new life He offered has liberated them from fear and an eternity of darkness.